Praise

How should Christian parents, pastors, and leaders approach issues of sexuality with the next generation? In a desire to correct unhelpful models of purity, many are hesitant or even hostile to teaching the Bible's countercultural ethic of sexuality. Dean Inserra offers a courageous but pastoral correction to this worrisome trend, offering Christians a road map to helping young people see the richness of God's plan for a flourishing marriage and sexuality. In a world where our kids are bombarded by mixed messages, parents must be intentional. This is a resource that every pastor, youth pastor, college pastor, and parent should have in bulk.

DANIEL DARLING, director of the Land Center for Cultural Engagement at Southwestern Seminary and bestselling author of several books, including *The Dignity Revolution, A Way With Words,* and *The Characters of Christmas*

I've seen the purity pendulum swing wildly over the years. There's no question that the way many of us as Christians have reacted to the sexual libertarianism of our culture has left many people shamed and scarred. But as Dean Inserra shows in this compelling book, God's design for our sexuality is both clear and good. I am thankful for this call to holiness and purity that is full of both grace and truth.

BOB LEPINE, long-time cohost of *FamilyLife Today*; author, *Love Like You Mean It*; pastor, Redeemer Community Church of Little Rock

Is it possible to live out a healthy, biblical, distinctively Christian sexual ethic in today's world? What about all of the excesses of "purity culture"? Is the very idea of sexual purity antiquated? Or even harmful? In *Pure,* Dean Inserra deals directly with the problems of the purity movement while clearly articulating God's design for sex. As always, Dean's work is accessible, humorous, and grounded in Scripture. This book is an excellent resource for teenagers, parents, and all who work with them.

JIMMY & KRISTIN SCROGGINS, authors of *Full-Circle Parenting*

Looking back on any hugely popular trend or phenomenon in our culture—or in the church—the benefit of time lets us see possible gaps and weaknesses. Regardless of your opinion about sexual purity campaigns of the past, Dean Inserra has compiled a helpful book that points to the full picture of why God created sex and the context for which it was intended. In short, we must not let possible shortcomings from past emphases lead us to anything less than a scriptural view of love, marriage, and sex that God has given us in His Word.

KEVIN EZELL, president, North American Mission Board, SBC

Contemporary evangelicalism is obsessed with social justice and loving one's neighbor. But when it comes to the topic that is literally destroying people's lives inside and outside the church, sexuality, so few are willing to speak up. Dean Inserra's *Pure* is. So few are as willing to be as clear, bold, and unapologetic about the Bible's witness on sexuality as Dean, and that's chiefly because Dean believes biblical sexuality is for our good, not for our harm or for repressing our desires. If the church is to love its neighbor and seek society's welfare, there are few more practical ways to do so than to the tell the truth about God's design for sexuality.

ANDREW T. WALKER, Associate Professor of Christian Ethics, The Southern Baptist Theological Seminary; fellow, The Ethics and Public Policy Center

Dean Inserra has done it again! He has given Christians another resource to help us navigate the critical issues we face today. This time he tackles the "purity culture" and gives us a better way to think about all things related to dating, marriage, and sex. This is what *Pure* is all about. With his quick wit and keen theological insight, Inserra calls believers to a higher and more holy standard regarding the way we think about our purity and operate in our personal relationships. Written from the heart of a pastor, Dean strikes the perfect balance of calling out sin and communicating hard truths in a spirit of grace and love. This book is going to challenge, encourage, and help a lot of people. I highly recommend it.

JARRETT STEPHENS, Senior Pastor at Champion Forest Baptist Church and author of *The Always God: He Hasn't Changed and You Are Not Forgotten*

For those of us who grew up in the midst of the purity culture movement and are now watching the backlash against it online and in real life, Dean Inserra's *Pure* is a helpful resource. What does the Bible really say about sex? Why should Christians commit to purity? What does a biblical sexual ethic actually look like in today's culture? This book answers those questions and more. Whether you are married or single, questioning the lessons of purity culture or ministering to those who are, this book provides a gracious and unapologetic look at what the Bible has to say about God's design for us.

ELIZABETH HYNDMAN, Editorial Project Leader, Lifeway Women

In a world crazed and confused by sex, and in a church culture increasingly embarrassed by and open to redefining the clear sexual ethics of the Bible, I cannot think of a more important book than Dean Inserra's *Pure.* Dean does not dodge a single critical issue, and he handles them all—including "kissing dating goodbye," "true love waits," "gay is okay," and "porn is the norm"—with biblical truth, pastoral compassion, and timely relevance. And as usual, the Inserra wit makes the book easy to read! Everyone should get this book and wrestle with its important message!

JONATHAN AKIN, Vice President for Church Relations and Campus Ministries, Carson-Newman University

We live in a deeply confused age, one that worships hyperindividualism and its "anything goes" approach to sexuality and valorizes religious deconstruction and its suspicion of authority. Dean Inserra's straightforward clarity cuts through that confusion by refocusing us on the purpose of a Christian sexual ethic: to be faithful followers of Jesus. In characteristic fashion, he shies away from nothing, confronting false and unfulfilling narratives both in, and out of, the American church. "When we break God's design, we should expect brokenness, not bliss." Pastor Inserra calls us to realign ourselves—body, soul, and spirit—with the One who designed our sexuality and heals our brokenness. This call goes beyond correcting "purity culture" or its subsequent pendulum swings to describe a discipleship that is holistically and single-mindedly pure.

KATIE J. MCCOY, Director, Women's Ministry, Center for Church Health

Unlike so many think pieces regarding purity culture, Inserra grounds his critique in biblical rather than worldly wisdom, then offers practical, Bible-based advice for a better way to approach dating, marriage, and sex. More than just a look at the purity craze of the nineties, this charitable work offers the ancillary impact of causing us to look more closely at today's fad answers to sin.

MEGAN BASHAM, *The Daily Wire*

WHY THE
BIBLE'S
PLAN FOR
SEXUALITY

ISN'T
OUTDATED,
IRRELEVANT,
OR OPPRESSIVE

DEAN
INSERRA

MOODY PUBLISHERS

CHICAGO

Some content in this book was adapted from previously published content on the author's website, erlc.com, and adflegal.org.

Scripture quotations have been taken from the Christian Standard Bible®, Copyright © 2017 by Holman Bible Publishers. Used by permission. Christian Standard Bible® and CSB® are federally registered trademarks of Holman Bible Publishers.

Names and details of some stories have been changed to protect the privacy of individuals.

Edited by Charles Snyder
Interior design: Brandi Davis
Cover design: Erik M. Peterson
Cover illustration of man silhouette copyright © 2020 by Design GENESIS / Lightstock (647386). All rights reserved.

ISBN: 978-0-8024-2308-5

Originally delivered by fleets of horse-drawn wagons, the affordable paperbacks from D. L. Moody's publishing house resourced the church and served everyday people. Now, after more than 125 years of publishing and ministry, Moody Publishers' mission remains the same—even if our delivery systems have changed a bit. For more information on other books (and resources) created from a biblical perspective, go to www.moodypublishers.com or write to:

Moody Publishers
820 N. LaSalle Boulevard
Chicago, IL 60610

1 3 5 7 9 10 8 6 4 2

Printed in the United States of America

Contents

SECTION

Setting
the Stage

1

Purity Culture & "True Love Waits"

If you want to start a riot among many young adult Christians, mention the words "purity culture." It's a "trigger" comparable to talking politics with your uncle over Thanksgiving dinner or yelling "Go Yankees!" at Fenway Park. The angst runs deep. Gospel Coalition editor Joe Carter defines purity culture as "the term often used for the evangelical movement that attempts to promote a biblical view of purity . . . by discouraging dating and promoting virginity before marriage, often through the use of tools such as purity pledges, symbols such as purity rings, and events such as purity balls."[1]

While a biblical view of purity seems like something Christians should easily affirm, parts of the 1990s youth ministry movement are now considered extremist and damaging to an entire generation. While I never attended a purity ball (thanks Mom and Dad), I was immersed in the movement without even realizing it, simply by attending and participating in evangelical youth events and ministries. Those of us who came to faith or came of age as Christians during the 1990s had little understanding that one day our peers would look back with contempt at this phenomenon that emphasized the importance of sexual abstinence until marriage.

Some believe that a harsh focus on abstinence fueled a backlash of suppressed sexual addiction. After one recent horrific incident, a shooter attributed his killing of several women to his own sex addiction, which one writer comments is "an assertion many in the evangelical world recognize as an outgrowth of purity culture gone awry."[2] Others focus on the shame that stemmed from inadequately maintaining the outward expressions of commitment taught in the movement.[3] In an opinion piece for the *New York Times*, Katelyn Beaty wrote that "purity culture as it was taught to my generation hurt many people and kept them from knowing the loving, merciful God at the heart of Christian faith," and was a "psychological burden that many of my peers and I are still unloading."[4]

Nevertheless, the movement began with good intentions, hoping to provide an alternative to the sexual revolution and "safe sex" campaigning taking place across the country. Carter helps place the movement in the context of the era:

> The purity culture movement began in the 1990s as Christians who were children or teens during the beginning of the 1960s-era sexual revolution began to have children and teenagers of their own. By the early years of 1990s, AIDS had become the number one cause of death[5] for United States men ages 25 to 44, and the teen pregnancy rate had reached an all-time high.[6] The number of premarital sex partners had also increased substantially since the 1970s.[7]

It is not radical to see those statistics as grounds for great concern or to desire an alternative to the mainstream message of the surrounding society regarding sex. Yet so many look back on the purity culture movement with anything from an eye roll to full trauma. To begin to understand this phenomenon, one must go back to 1993 and the True Love Waits pledge.

TAKING THE PLEDGE

In 1993, being a faithful Christian teenager in American evangelical life meant "taking the pledge." This was done by signing your name below the following statement on a card, indicating that you were making the promises of the card—a type of oath— to God, yourself, and your future spouse (known on the card as your mate).

"Believing that true love waits, I make a commitment to God, myself, my family, those I date, my future mate, and my future children to be sexually pure until the day I enter a covenant marriage relationship." [8]

Signing the True Love Waits card was second in significance only to walking the aisle at a church service (the means by which many give their lives to Jesus Christ in evangelical culture). The card wasn't something youth leaders randomly passed out and collected, as one might take an offering or distribute forms for an upcoming mission trip. This was a national initiative with all the bells and whistles. It resembled a Billy Graham evangelistic crusade, but rather than giving your life to Jesus and becoming born again, you committed to the card and its contents. Instead of walking the aisle to a song like "Just As I Am," you walked the aisle to a hypothetical future spouse whom you had never met but were making a pledge to at the age of fourteen—a promise to keep yourself a virgin for him or her. In 1994, True Love Waits [9] held a rally in Washington, DC, with twenty-five thousand youth, displaying more than two hundred thousand commitment cards from students across the country, more than double what the Southern Baptist convention had hoped to see. [10] Remaining a virgin until marriage was the goal and the promise, and families traveled to Washington, DC, to make the promise known.

It's no surprise that purity culture and the True Love Waits movement didn't "solve" sexual immorality issues among young people inside or outside the church. But given the fact that countless people have come forward in recent years to share their stories of how purity culture had adverse effects on them or led to their actual abuse, we should consider where it went wrong. I believe the movement was aiming to fix the wrong problem with the wrong solution. Let me explain.

God's design for sex and sexuality is good. The Bible tells the story of Adam and Eve and emphasizes their oneness: "A man leaves his father and mother and bonds with his wife, and they become one flesh. Both the man and his wife were naked, yet felt no shame" (Gen. 2:24–25). This becoming of one flesh is more than sexual intercourse, but it certainly isn't less. In the New Testament, both Jesus (in Matt. 19) and Paul (in Eph. 5) reference this union of Adam and Eve as God's design for sex and marriage, pointing to it as God's historical and right context for sex to exist and flourish. Here are a man and woman, created for each other, united as one flesh, and they are naked without any shame. How is it that a Christian movement intending to promote God's good design could stir up so many negative feelings and thoughts for a generation of Christians?

We need to look no further than the next chapter in Genesis to see the script flip. Suddenly, this first couple, the apex of God's good creation, gets entangled in pain and shame.

- Genesis 2:25: "Both the man and his wife were naked yet felt no shame."
- Genesis 3:7: "Then the eyes of both of them were opened, and they knew they were naked; so they sewed fig leaves together and made coverings for themselves."

In Genesis 2:25, nakedness carried zero shame. But I don't even have to turn the page in my Bible to see the exact same people, Adam and Eve, now realizing they were naked. Suddenly, they're busting out their sewing machines to cover themselves from each other. What happened that took us from no shame to frantically looking for clothes?

Sin.

The New City Catechism defines sin as "rejecting or ignoring God in the world he created, rebelling against him by living without reference to him, not being or doing what he requires in his law—resulting in our death and the disintegration of all creation."[11]

The Bible is clear that "the wages of sin is death" (Rom. 6:23), and certainly this includes physical death. The sin of Adam and Eve led to their expulsion from the garden of Eden and to certainty of their eventual death as people who had violated the command of the one true holy God. But this death also breaks, distorts, and poisons the people and things God created. When we reject the good commands of God, choosing what we desire instead, we enter a world that is not as it should be, and we see the decline of society and creation as a whole. Brokenness is the new reality of this world and the people who are banned from the garden of Eden.

Pastor Paul Carter says that "it would be hard to overstate the significance and impact of human sin—cosmically, corporately and personally. The effect of sin is not just an issue for the planet or for the species—it affects us profoundly as human beings."[12] Yes, sin effects everything. What strikes me about the Genesis story is that the very first thing we see affected is Adam and Eve's view of nakedness. The sequence of the events is striking: "She took some of its fruit and ate it; she also gave some to her husband, who was with her, and he ate it. Then the eyes of both of them were opened, and they knew they were naked; so they sewed fig leaves together and made coverings for themselves" (Gen. 3:6–7). Immediately after eating the fruit, Adam and Eve's eyes were opened to their nakedness and they felt shame. Sin brought brokenness into the good world that God had made, and the first apparent change was to the sexual aspects of their bodies. Even being naked in front of your own spouse didn't seem natural in this broken world.

Ever since this swift-yet-enormous shift, sin and its effects have gone full speed into the world, affecting every area of life. Sexual sin is a primary example of the fall's catastrophic consequences. Who would have thought that eating from a forbidden tree would usher in a world of adultery, pornography, sexual abuse, abortion, fatherlessness, homosexuality, hook-up culture, cohabitation, and an abundance of shame? Yet God is sovereign over the brokenness and warns His people against departing from His design. Like any good parent, He is specific about the danger and commands the Christian to flee from both the temptation and the action (1 Cor. 6:18).

Enter the True Love Waits movement, which focused on "saving yourself." The main reason for doing so was simple: your future spouse deserves it. I am not being unfair or making a broad swipe; this was the message. One's future spouse was idealized as the ultimate motivation. Not only does this approach fail to recognize the only remedy for sin (forgiveness in the blood of Christ and full cleansing to walk in newness of life), but it exalts the created instead of the Creator, which is the definition of idolatry seen in all of Scripture. What you received was God's design without God's glory or God's grace.

FORGIVEN? OR SECOND-CLASS CITIZEN?

I remember hearing about "secondary virginity" during the movement. This was for people who had already lost their virginity before signing the pledge card. It was a type of second chance. However, your future spouse would probably be very disappointed or feel cheated by your lack of previous commitment to the future marriage. Katelyn Beaty writes, "One piece of youth-group folklore was a 'game' in which a cup would be passed around a circle. At each turn, someone would spit in the cup, until the last person had a cup full of spit. 'Would you want to drink this?' the youth pastor intoned. 'No. And that's how others will see you if you sleep around.'"[13] I never saw or had heard of this activity, but the principle represented by that story was certainly taught. You needed to save yourself for marriage because you didn't want to be the one in your future marriage who wasn't a virgin.

Contemporary Christian music got behind the movement as popular 90s singer Rebecca St. James released the song "Wait For Me" toward the end of the True Love Waits craze in 2001. Five years after writing and releasing the song, she reflected, "It's a pretty well-known fact that guys would like to marry a virgin. I think the whole idea that a girl is singing that song and is waiting really appeals to them too and helps them to strive to be men of honor."[14] I have zero doubt that St. James was sincere concerning her hope that the song would encourage a generation of Christians trying to walk in sexual purity. I'm sure she had a positive impact on many through her music, but even the lyrics of the song are in sync with the focus of True Love Waits. The emphasis is on the unknown future spouse, not on honoring God, being surrendered to Him, and walking in the power of the Holy Spirit for whatever life God ordained for you.

I remember a friend in college who broke up with her boyfriend (who was a genuine follower of Christ) because she asked him if he was a virgin and he told her that he had had sex with his high school girlfriend after their junior prom. He answered her question honestly, and she broke up with him. The reason was that she had waited and didn't want to marry someone who hadn't. This was the generation raised in True Love Waits. It didn't matter that God had forgiven this young man; his failure made him ineligible in the mind of this young woman, as though he would never be as pure as she had been. The badge of honor in this culture was the card, symbolized by a purity ring around the finger, that one day would be handed over to a future spouse—a type of finish line and trophy ceremony disguised as a honeymoon for those who kept the pledge.

The purity culture of my youth launched a type of prosperity gospel wearing the disguise of piety. *If I remain a virgin until marriage, God will give me a future spouse who did the same. In fact, they don't deserve me if they failed to do what I did.* The aftermath of this anti-gospel thinking is a trail of human brokenness. There aren't enough fig leaves to cover up the damage. Imagine being a Christian teen who had succumbed to sexual sin in this culture, even one time. If you had committed the ultimate mistake of having sex, you had become damaged goods, so why quit now? What's done is done, right? So, in the next relationship, you could think, "I guess we will have sex, because I already lost my virginity, so what's the point now of abstaining?" The "secondary virgin" classification didn't seem to have mass appeal, so you might as well quit the race altogether.

At True Love Waits rallies, the testimonies were always, without fail, from college students or young adults (usually women) who had previously had sex outside of marriage and now were trying to do better as secondary virgins. The hope was that since God forgave them, maybe a future spouse would, too. Instead of championing the full and sufficient cleansing of Christ's atoning death, these poor people were often treating themselves as cautionary tales for a younger generation, urging others to not become like them. The invitation following the testimony would be to sign the

card. Picturing myself sitting in the bleachers of a gym and hearing that message, I remember my conclusion was always, "Gosh, I
hope my future wife doesn't mess up like she did, especially if I'm
gonna try to do this whole pledge thing. And I have to sign the
card because I'm not going to be the person in this room everyone
looks at with evil eyes if I don't!"

Purity culture walked into a world of sexual brokenness and
provided the solution of following the rules and practicing abstinence so you wouldn't be the one on your future honeymoon
who lost in the game. Is this what God had in mind at His creation
of humanity? Certainly not.

What began as a good and worthy endeavor inadvertently
produced Pharisees on one side of the True Love Waits card and
people desperately grasping for fig leaves on the other. "Rather
than emphasize the gift of sex within marriage, purity culture typically led with the shame of having sex outside of it."[15] It is easy
to play Monday morning quarterback and critique, yet the play-
book was the biggest problem. Virginity does not provide moral
superiority, nor does past sexual sin doom someone to finding a
lesser spouse. We don't pursue abstinence from sex apart from
marriage because someone we might marry one day "deserves it."
We reserve sex for marriage because God has a design. When we
depart from that design, we find more brokenness. This brokenness creeps into many of our relationships with other people. But,
most importantly, it affects our relationship with God.

Something we must not overlook from the garden of Eden
story is that the clothes Adam and Eve would use to cover themselves were provided by God Himself (Gen. 3:21). God is the
healer of our shame, and the story after the fatal sin in the garden
is one of recovery and pursuit of God's design in the lives of His
people and in His world.

God not only made new outfits for Adam and Eve, He made a

promise. Those clothes would only last so long, and Adam and Eve didn't simply need their guilt and shame covered—they would need it removed. The consequences would be great.

> I will put hostility between you and the woman,
> and between your offspring and her offspring.
> He will strike your head,
> and you will strike his heel. (Gen. 3:15)

> The LORD God said, "Since the man has become like one of us, knowing good and evil, he must not reach out, take from the tree of life, eat, and live forever." So the LORD God sent him away from the garden of Eden to work the ground from which he was taken. He drove the man out and stationed the cherubim and the flaming, whirling sword east of the garden of Eden to guard the way to the tree of life. (Gen. 3:22–24)

There was banishment and consequence, but there was also hope. From the offspring of this couple would one day come a Savior who would strike the head of the serpent by being struck Himself. Jesus Christ, born of a woman, would enter the brokenness of humanity, but never sin. He would take on the wages of sin and bring about a future restoration of all broken things by dying on a cross, rising from the grave, ascending to heaven, and coming back to establish a permanent kingdom where no darkness exists. In the meantime, God still has a design and an ethic for His people: to live as lights shining to a broken world.

WHAT NOW?

I fear we are experiencing an overcorrection to the failures and flaws of purity culture. Missteps by fallible human people do not erase or alter the infallible design of the holy and perfect Creator.

I have always thought the saying "don't throw the baby out with the bath water" sounded weird, but it is the appropriate expression to describe what is happening among certain Christians regarding sexual ethics. We're not simply correcting the flaws of purity culture and pursuing a different path of truth and grace. No, professing Christians are living with their boyfriend or girlfriend, affirming same-sex marriage, laughing at any call to modesty, and agreeing with a surrounding sexual revolution that God's design found in the Bible is outdated or even oppressive. The church has a challenge in front of her if we are going to be faithful in not only declaring the whole counsel of God but also walking as faithful disciples, pointing a lost and broken world to a design that is for God's glory, and for their good.

We must figure out how to uphold sexual ethics in not simply an anti-purity culture world, but amongst anti-purity culture Christians. Waving the white flag of surrender over something so clear and precious in Scripture as God's design for sex and marriage cannot be the answer to correcting purity culture. The answer is to recover and pursue God's design as He continues to restore a broken people to Himself, and to believe that this is far better than what any pledge card or deserving spouse has to offer.

God has a design and an ethic. We do not find it in purity culture, but in His Word.

2

Purity Culture &
"I Kissed Dating Goodbye"

I know book banning is bad, but as a teenage boy, I would have
been all for the practice. Let me explain. In my public high school,
there were only so many committed Christian girls. I knew all their
names. You know, for like-minded companionship. Okay, mostly
because I wanted a girlfriend. One morning at school, I asked one
of these girls if she wanted to go off campus for lunch with me.
It was a JV-level date where you went somewhere casual together,
like on a drive-through burger run. She told me that sounded fine,
and she would come with me, but there was a catch. I needed to
know she wasn't going to date until she got married. She went on
to explain that her small group at church read a book called *I Kissed
Dating Goodbye*,[1] and they had all committed together that they
would no longer date anyone. In that moment, I was ready to find a
copy of this book and punt it across the school parking lot.

If purity culture had a sacred text, it was *I Kissed Dating Goodbye*. Written by then-twenty-one-year-old Joshua Harris, the book

promoted what he called "courting" as an alternative to dating. A quarter-century removed from the book, I still do not know exactly what courting means, but Harris explained it all the way to more than one million copies sold. Every—and I mean every—teenage girl from an evangelical family during the purity culture era read the book. I can speak for a lot of late 1990s Christian teenage guys when I say just hearing the name of that book still makes me roll my eyes. It gave the girls an easy out from adolescent, immature boys, but they ate it up, and I wanted the book banned.

I Kissed Dating Goodbye has taken an interesting journey since its heyday. Harris now denounces the message of the book and no longer identifies as a Christian. He would go on to eventually critique his own book and star in a documentary called, "I Survived I Kissed Dating Goodbye."[2] Me too, Josh. Me too. Harris has apologized for his book, confessing his remorse to those it negatively affected. I can't claim to be one of those people; I was just a boy who was mad the Christian girl group at my school made a "just say no" to dating pact. Hardly traumatizing, just annoying! But what would cause someone to say the book caused them actual pain? The easy answer is that much of popular evangelicalism is driven by fads. When this book came on the scene, its wave washed over an entire generation. But there is much more to the *I Kissed Dating Goodbye* phenomenon than popularity. The opening paragraph of Harris's book sets the stage:

> It was finally here—Anna's wedding day, the day she had dreamed about and planned for months. The small, picturesque church was crowded with friends and family. . . . But as the minister began to lead Anna and David through their vows, the unthinkable happened. A girl stood up in the middle of the congregation, walked quietly to the altar, and took David's other hand. Another girl approached and

stood next to the first, followed by another. Soon, a chain of six girls stood by him as he repeated his vows to Anna. . . . "Is this some kind of joke?" she whispered to David. "I'm . . . I'm sorry, Anna," he said, staring at the floor. "Who are these girls, David? What is going on?" she gasped. "They're girls from my past. . . . Anna, they don't mean anything to me now, but I've given part of my heart to each of them."[3]

Out of the gate, the looming threat is sins from one's past, literally presented as unwelcome, intrusive guests ruining a wedding day and traumatizing a young bride. In this scene, the triumph of the gospel would seem out of place, but it correctly reflects the cautionary tale of much of purity culture, including True Love Waits, with its preeminent goal of not having regret on your wedding day. While Harris does write a very helpful and gospel-filled chapter about forgiveness in Christ elsewhere in the book, the unofficial premise remains, "Don't mess things up for your honeymoon." However, it's not necessarily healthy to assume that a honeymoon is constantly on the radar of a sixteen-year-old. What should regularly be on the mind of a Christian is God and His Word. That alone should be motivation to fight sin. Walking with God is not a hypothetical future dream (unlike a honeymoon, which is not a guarantee for anyone). His presence through His Word is available to us now, on demand, always in front of us.

> **Why is dating complicated for Christians? The Bible doesn't talk about it.**

Dating is something that purity culture has never been able to figure out. Actually, American Christianity in general hasn't figured it out either. Why is dating complicated for Christians? The Bible doesn't talk about it. The Bible talks about sexual ethics and about marriage and engagement, but there is no prescriptive category for dating or having a boyfriend or girlfriend in the Scriptures. That doesn't make dating wrong, just unclear. Since we don't have a clear dating example from Scripture, this category has been, and has to be, invented. But it must occur within the non-negotiables we do find in Scripture. Harris—as a twenty-one-year-old—essentially wrote the dating rules for evangelicals at that time. But even for himself, those rules didn't last. Eventually he met someone and they got married. And you can call it courting, but, in reality, it's dating.

In modern-day Western culture, the road to marriage typically begins with a pseudo-committed relationship which progresses through dating. It often begins with two people going on a casual date or two to get to know each other. Then it usually progresses to exclusive dating. For many Christians, this is the unofficially sanctioned system for finding the person you are going to marry. We must figure out how to faithfully navigate, as "strangers and exiles" (1 Peter 2:11), a process created by this world. I do believe Harris was trying to help Christians do exactly that, but his approach was flawed and ultimately didn't work.

Yet buried in the book's message is something worth recovering. If there is an area of life where there isn't enough distinction between Christians and non-Christians, it's arguably the category we call "dating." I'm referring to the exclusive, serious relationships that individuals usually engage in with several different people before they get married. Prior to the sexual revolution, men would pursue a woman toward marriage. Nowadays, a man pursues a woman toward a dating relationship. That isn't necessarily a bad thing. It just makes things quite complicated for the Christian who is trying to live his or her life in holiness, because the category of dating is something we invented. The Bible doesn't even acknowledge it. Relationship statuses in the Bible are almost exclusively presented as married or single. Widows are certainly mentioned and given a great place of care in the Scriptures, but being widowed isn't exactly its own unique relationship category (widows, like other singles, are free to marry or remain single). We also see mention of one being betrothed, most famously in the case of Mary and Joseph in the Gospels, a status which roughly parallels our understanding of engagement. But "boyfriends" and "girlfriends" and being "committed" to someone who is not your spouse are all foreign to God's design.

Paul wrote that when we are in sexual sin, we look like people "who don't know God" (1 Thess. 4:5). Dating makes this complicated, because it constructs regular and increasingly more tempting opportunities to operate like people who don't know God. So, what is one to do? Purity-culture-era Harris would urge Christians to abandon the practice altogether. My approach is different. I believe dating can be a healthy part of the Christian life. As Christians, however, our dating should be distinct from the world and conducted in a God-honoring manner. I call it "no regrets dating."

Let's go back to Harris's opening illustration about the wedding day and David's apology to Anna. "They're girls from my past. Anna, they don't mean anything to me now, but I've given part of my heart to each of them." Does all of that really have to happen when you date? In another chapter, I present from Scripture how sex certainly gives a part of yourself to someone, as that is what it is designed to do. But do dating relationships have to be that intense, especially without sex? To be fair, Harris is using an exaggerated hypothetical example, but it is the opening premise of the book. His suggested response is to kiss dating goodbye by encouraging "courting." I understand courting to mean that a couple enters a relationship with clear intentions for and expectations of marriage. I assume they were "just friends" and then decided otherwise, but nonetheless, they are in a relationship that is exclusive, but is not marriage (so, sort of the same flaws as dating but with even more pressure). This approach makes dating way more intense than it has to be and could make people give their hearts away more deeply than in a non-courting relationship. But I'm a realistic person, and I think the approach of courting is a pipe dream that sounds great on paper but isn't a reality for most Christian singles.

Given that we are not provided with a biblical script for our cultural creation of dating, I believe "no regrets dating" is the best approach. Dating is a prevalent part of our culture and a modern-day prerequisite for engagement, so we must learn how to approach it as Christians. The answer is not to "kiss dating goodbye" or try to overhaul a central component of our society, but rather to embrace the fact that following Jesus will interfere with our lives—even our dating lives—and that this should cause us to approach relationships differently. Again, as Paul said to the Thessalonians, we should not act like those who do not know God. "No regrets dating" can be summed up in four guidelines.

1. STOP ACTING LIKE YOU'RE MARRIED WHEN YOU ARE NOT.

We tend to treat exclusive dating relationships as though they are quasi-marriages, giving them a measure of security that God never intended (and that isn't really there). For the Christian, if the only thing that changes when you get married is that you start having sex, something is wrong. When we read the common thread of Scripture, from Genesis to Jesus to Paul, we read that "a man will leave his father and mother and be joined to his wife, and the two will become one flesh . . . so they are no longer two, but one flesh" (Matt. 19:5–6). Should we really be giving ourselves away emotionally and romantically to someone who is not our spouse? To give credit where credit is due, I think Harris was right in this regard. Giving your heart away four or five times by the age of twenty-seven is not healthy. When a dating couple functions as a package deal—when they give joint presents at parties, post the equivalent of engagement pictures on social media, and declare anniversaries of their "define the relationship" conversation—they mirror the world's idea of casually-committed relationships, declaring a pretend marriage that God does not recognize. The world at large may exhibit this kind of boundary-pushing union with sex, cohabitation, etc., but this can (and does) happen within the church, even among couples who abstain from sex before marriage.

There must be a better way to date than acting as a married couple minus sex. Especially because we've seen that many Christians have entered these kinds of relationships with several different people. Making out with someone every night and saying "I love you" is not what we find in the Scriptures for the unmarried. That's not really a brother/sister-in-Christ relationship. I can't see how Christians can make the case that a sort of quasi-marriage should happen with multiple partners in a lifetime. There is a way to still date someone and not be so intense. And this intensity can exist even if there isn't sexual tension present—think of the sweet Christian boyfriend and girlfriend who come as a package deal. If you invite one to your house for dinner, it means you invite both; they learn each other's "love languages,"[4] travel, and "do" all the holidays together. They aren't around their friends as much anymore, and if they are, the other is with them. If that relationship ends, there will be regrets. So much time given, life altered, and emotion invested. It is also essential to understand that the boyfriend is not the leader in the relationship. That is a duty reserved for husbands. A boyfriend should not have pressure placed on him to be a "spiritual leader" in a dating relationship, nor should a girlfriend feel any obligation to be under his leadership. The practice instead should be two individuals who treat each other as siblings in Christ, because this is the category Scripture places them under as unmarried men and women. So, to sum it up, pump the brakes and chill out.

2. MAKE INTENTIONS KNOWN IN DATING.

Vocalizing your intentions is not the same as courting; it's being considerate of the other person. To the eager guys, don't freak a girl out by bringing up marriage during your first conversation. Nonetheless, you should exercise clarity and be intentional. Here is what that looks like:

- Intentional: "I'd like to take you out on a date. Are you free next weekend?"
- Unintentional: "Wanna hang out sometime?" (Extra loser points if you take this road and then try to kiss her at the end of the night.)

Intentional clarity allows the man and woman to know what is or is not happening. If you think it is a date, and the other person thinks you're just hanging out as friends, you are creating weirdness from the start. If intentions are clear, and the first date goes well (leading to a couple more dates), then you can start to ask basic questions that will provide helpful answers. If the guy or girl you are dating says, "I don't want to get engaged until after grad school," and you aren't planning on waiting that long for what could or could not happen with the relationship, you can say "no thanks," and nobody is mad or taken advantage of because intentions were made known. An awkward conversation about intentions at the beginning is much better than heartbreak later.

3. FOREPLAY IS NOT IN PLAY.

There is one purpose and one purpose only for what is known as "foreplay." (I don't even think anyone calls it that anymore, but I'm going with it because it seems the most appropriate.) Its purpose is to prepare you for and lead you to sexual intercourse. It was not designed to stop before a climax. Foreplay between two unmarried people is absolutely what the Scriptures would designate as "sexual immorality." You must put standards in place—my best advice is that when the date is over, the date is over. Guys, walk her to the door, drop her off, and go home. If there are other people there, sure, go inside. If not, know yourself and where you are tempted and be wise! Jesus said, "If your right hand causes you to sin, cut it off and throw it away. For it is better that you lose one of the parts of your body than for your whole body to go into hell" (Matt. 5:30)! Better to do something as non-sacrificial as cutting the night off early than to sin.

Christians must get serious about sexual sin. Sex, foreplay, nakedness, etc. are not for dating people, in-love people, or mature people, but for married people. One does not have to kiss dating goodbye to understand this. In the world's idea of dating, sex is expected. Taking that off the table immediately in a dating relationship sets a man and woman up to have no regrets if a breakup eventually happens, because they treated each other first as brother and sister in Christ.

4. REALIZE THAT YOU ARE NOT REALLY COMMITTED.

There are two things that can happen when you date: either you get married, or you break up. Not counting unexpected tragedies, every dating relationship either ends with a breakup conversation or results in a wedding. So please understand, if you are in an exclusive dating relationship, you are not bound by it or forced to stay in it. The biblical boundaries for marriage and divorce don't apply here. What does it really mean to be committed in dating, anyways? It means that you are committed until one of you decides you aren't anymore.

It reminds me of college football recruiting. Few things get college football fans to pay attention to every waking moment of a high school kid's life other than when their favorite team is recruiting a star player. The goal of the coaching staff is to get that player to commit to their school. But even after the high school athlete commits, he can still change his mind until national signing day, when he signs an official letter of intent. A player announcing his commitment to a certain school creates a frenzy among its fan base, but his commitment isn't really a commitment. It's all pretend until the student athlete signs his name on the dotted line. It is commonplace in the college football recruiting world for someone to claim he is a "soft commitment." Yes, he is committed to Auburn, but he's still checking out Alabama and Clemson. He is committed, but not so much.

This is dating in a nutshell. You are in a committed relationship unless and until one of you decides otherwise. That is perfectly okay. In fact, it's a good thing. There is no biblically binding commitment for a dating couple, even an engaged couple! You might be labeled a bad guy, lose your deposit on a reception venue, or realize you spent way too much money on Valentine's Day, but you are simply a "soft commitment" until you sign your letter of intent by getting married. This is how dating should be viewed. You should never feel stuck or trapped in a dating relationship. Chances are, the more emotional and physical intimacy that is exchanged, the more you will feel stuck. The reality is that God does not tell us in His Word that a boyfriend and girlfriend are His design and that nobody should separate the two. That claim is reserved for marriage. You can call it dating or courting, but it still applies the same; it is a house of cards commitment that isn't binding.

Married Christians should keep this in mind when walking through life with other believers who are dating or engaged. Dating is a time to evaluate the character of another person, and godly community should be part of that, but we shouldn't treat our dating friends like they are married or make them feel guilty about getting out of a dating relationship that isn't headed towards marriage. What a shame if church community is the reason someone feels like he or she can't rightfully end a dating relationship.

TO THE STILL-IN-WAITING

I am not a big fan of *I Kissed Dating Goodbye*, and not because of some old bitterness from high school. My wife read the book, and thankfully never treated it as inspired Scripture. Neither of us are casualties of *I Kissed Dating Goodbye*. We met, liked each other, started dating, got engaged a year later, and then married. We followed the conventional, modern Western process. However, some would consider themselves casualties of the book and its message, and that pain is part of the difficulty in talking about dating and sexuality in an American evangelical context. If any individuals feel shame and guilt based on judgement cast upon them from the purity culture craze, I truly hope they can find their worth in Christ rather than in legalism or a former Christian movement. But for others who imagine themselves as victims because Harris and others' promises didn't come true, there may be a bit of self-pity coming into play and a need for gospel perspective. Perhaps you were taught that being a "lady in waiting" meant that a sexually pure Christian Prince Charming would be waiting for you. Or perhaps you got mocked on the football team for choosing not to sleep around. Maybe those classmates who made a mockery of your decisions got married, and here you are, single and tired of being told to mingle, never having the chance to meet that right person.

A great deal of the Christian life is fighting off the temptation to believe even the most subtle forms of the prosperity gospel. Besides being a false gospel, the great danger of the prosperity gospel is that it holds God to promises He never actually made. The True Love Waits and purity culture movements were not of prosperity gospel origin, but, perhaps unwittingly, their message created a belief among a generation of Christians that if they followed the rules, God would reward them with a spouse who had done the same. They would meet the right person, be married out of college, have the perfect honeymoon, and live a full life. If that's your assumption, and if those things haven't happened yet, it might be easy to blame purity culture. But don't forget that God's Word was probably just as readily available to you as Harris's word. However well-intentioned, Harris was writing about something he could not have had adequate experience in as a twenty-one-year-old unmarried man. But no matter the book's faults, it doesn't have any bearing on what God has said regarding marriage and sex. It is time for Christians raised in the purity culture movement to abandon futile attempts to undo its damage with angst-fueled public outrage and instead to pursue God's design for sexuality and marriage, while believing that God's ultimate goal in making us wait is to give us Himself.[5]

3

The Counter Swing
to "It's Just Sex"

If there is a definitive statement that explains Western society's
attitude toward sex, it would be that simple-yet-revealing claim:
"It's just sex." The only remaining boundaries regarding sex in our
society today are consent and not leveraging one's institutional
power for the purposes of sex. As long as you don't abuse power
and you receive consent from any and all involved, you are free to
operate according to the mantra of our day. Sex is now expected
not only in the realm of dating but even in an evening out on the
town, after meeting someone for the very first time. As a pastor in
a college town, I know students who pack an overnight bag before
going out on a Friday night, because on any given evening out
with friends, sex is a possibility. Richard E. Simmons III wrote
a book on this modern-day approach to sex and calls it "sex at
first sight." He shares the story of a recent college graduate who
recounted, "Sex pervades almost every aspect of dorm life that I
have experienced. I have seen 'dorm incest' where the entire floor

hooks up with everyone else on the floor."[1] To many students, sex is just part of the college experience.

I find it interesting that the "it's just sex" belief system contradicts itself out of the gate. It fails to acknowledge that even the idea of *consent amongst adults* points to an important reality. If you must agree to it and you must be old enough that your consent is viable, then sex means something. Abuse runs rampant in our sinful society, and few things rightly create more outrage among sane people than witnessing abuse. It is so serious that we refer to victims as "survivors," and all who believe that people are made in the image of God should be heartbroken and motivated to care well for those who have been victimized by the evils of abuse. Abuse cover-ups disgust people, and while there is certainly a long way to go toward changing the culture of abuse that exists in many spheres of life, outrage leading to action is finally starting to emerge due to survivors bravely coming forward to share their traumatic experiences. Once in the open, abuse usually receives the response it warrants, because people inherently know that sex is not to be taken by force.

I tread lightly as I explain this, but as hideous and horrific as non-sexual domestic abuse is, our responses to sexual abuse inherently convey that it is in a class of its own. I do not intend to minimize the trauma of domestic abuse in any manner. But in terms of both criminal consequences and general perception, rape or sexual abuse of any kind undeniably creates a different emotional response in our society. We know that sex coerced or taken is an evil thing. Sexual abuse is such a horrific departure from God's design that even an unbelieving world can call it sinful.

Let's delicately dial that back. Why is sex taken by force so disgusting? Because sex means something.

If it's "just sex," why would one need to give the disclaimer of consent? If a CEO of an organization is leveraging sex as a condition for job security or advancement in a company, or if a story breaks that a high school teacher is using his or her power abusively over a vulnerable student by having a sexual relationship, why does that outrage even the most secular mind? Because, in our gut, we know that "it's just sex" is a lie. Sex outside of God's design not only leads to brokenness but can also leave traumatized victims along the way. Sex is that serious, and the Bible is crystal clear in showing how ultimately catastrophic it is to take what God has given His people to enjoy and abuse it.

One important Scriptural argument against "it's just sex" is found in 1 Corinthians chapter six. In his letter to the church in Corinth, Paul confronts a departure from God's design for sex with a strong rebuke. It is not simply that they are having sex. Christian men had blended their faith with the pagan religions of their city and believed they could justify engaging in prostitution at the temple as acceptable religious activity. You read that correctly: professing Christians were having sex with prostitutes at a pagan temple.

To address the Corinthians' sin, Paul builds his argument incrementally. He first writes that sexual immorality is not the purpose of our bodies, saying, "the body is not for sexual immorality but for the Lord, and the Lord for the body," (1 Cor. 6:13). That element is easy to understand—since my body belongs to Christ, I shouldn't have sex with a prostitute. Got it. (Christians abstaining from prostitution is hardly a hot take.) Paul could have advised the church against prostitution for several reasons that would have made perfect sense, but instead he takes it somewhere otherworldly. He continues, "Don't you know that your bodies are a part of Christ's body? So should I take a part of Christ's body and make it part of a prostitute? Absolutely not" (6:15). He lands the plane in verse sixteen, where he lets the reader understand that his issues have nothing to do with prostitution but with what is taking place in the act of sex itself: "Don't you know that anyone joined to a prostitute is one body with her? For Scripture says, 'The two will become one flesh.'" Paul makes his appeal to the garden of Eden, to God's design for sex and what happens when sexual intercourse takes place.

"This is why a man leaves his father and mother and bonds with his wife, and they become one flesh. Both the man and his wife were naked, yet felt no shame" (Gen. 2:24–25). This is not about soliciting prostitutes; this is about God's design—when two come together, they become one. Let's be real—besides some hurt feelings, there are rarely deep scars after a breakup between a boyfriend and girlfriend who only ever cuddled on the couch watching a movie. But regardless of what the world tries to proclaim, there is much more to the emotional aftermath of a breakup when sex has been part of the relationship. Why? Paul points us to the beginning: the two become one flesh. Because the bond that sex creates between two people is so deep, there is trauma associated with sexual misconduct. Prostitution was simply the specific sin the Corinthians were committing. Yet Paul's argument had nothing to do with the method of their sexual immorality but with what sex actually is—the bringing together of not simply two bodies, but two souls.

> When we sin sexually, we sin against our own bodies, which God created and Jesus bought with the price of His own life.

It is from deep love, then, when Paul concludes his section on sexual sin by pleading with the believers to "flee sexual immorality" (1 Cor. 6:18). I can visualize his pen shaking in urgency as he wrote, "Every other sin a person commits is outside the body, but the person who is sexually immoral sins against his own body. Don't you know that your body is a temple of the Holy Spirit who is in you, whom you have from God? You are not your own, for you were bought at a price. So glorify God with your body" (6:18–20).

Paul does not seem to subscribe to the claim that all sins are equal in the eyes of God. All sin is an offense against God and requires full atonement made possible only through the death and resurrection of Jesus Christ, but sexual sin seems to be differentiated here as having a unique kind of consequence. When we sin sexually, we sin against our own bodies, which God created and Jesus bought with the price of His own life. Our physical bodies are temples of the Holy Spirit. In this context, Paul is not talking about wellness, diet plans, not eating too much sugar, or the need to do yoga. He is talking about sex. The act of sex unites the body and soul to someone else. Whether it's with a prostitute at the Corinthian temple, a boyfriend or girlfriend, or your spouse, this union is the reality.

Yet Paul gives a lifeline of hope that is easy to overlook in the weight of everything else he is communicating. He pivots briefly from talking about becoming one flesh in the act of sex to a different and greater union: "But anyone joined to the Lord is one spirit with him" (1 Cor. 6:17). In this broken Corinthian culture, Paul points the believers away from sexual immorality to their union with Christ. In his appeals to Genesis and to the believers' union with Christ, Paul wants them to realize the original intention of God the designer.

Like many of God's creations, sex has physical, practical reasons for existence as well as spiritual, poetic reasons. Was sex created for the purpose of procreation in order to populate the earth? Certainly, as Adam and Eve were told to be fruitful and multiply (Gen. 1:28). In addition, sex was created for pleasure and the mutual enjoyment of the husband and wife together (Prov. 5:18–19; 1 Cor. 7:5). But sex was also designed to create a oneness in marriage that points us to something greater. This oneness is not physically seen, like offspring, or merely felt, like sexual pleasure. The oneness of a husband and wife as one flesh is a physical understanding of a spiritual reality: our union with Christ. That can sound strange, but it is important to know that when God created marriage, He had the gospel in mind.

We see visual examples of spiritual realities all around us, as God has graciously given us human means to understand His divine love.

- When a child is adopted into a family, we are given a tangible portrait of our being adopted by our Heavenly Father in Christ.
- When I forgive someone who has wronged me, it points to the spiritual reality that God has forgiven me when I have sinned against Him.
- When a shepherd cares for his sheep, it is an image of how the Lord is our shepherd and we are His sheep.

Likewise, when God created marriage and Adam and Eve were united as one flesh, the joining of their bodies points us to the invisible, spiritual reality of Christ and the church, our union with Him.

John Murray wrote that "union with Christ is . . . the central truth of the whole doctrine of salvation."[2] Salvation in Christ accomplishes for us a marriage covenant. Justin Taylor helpfully explains we are in Christ and Christ is in us (John 6:56; John 15:4; 1 John 4:13).[3] Tony Reinke, commenting on Richard Gaffin's 2006 lecture "Union with Christ in the New Testament," states, "It is mystical union because it involves a great mystery, a mystery that has its closest analogy in the relationship between a husband and a wife."[4]

Paul understood the connection between sex and spiritual union when he rebuked the Corinthian church, and he wrote similar instructions with a totally different context to the Ephesian church. "For this reason a man will leave his father and mother and be joined to his wife, and the two will become one flesh. This mystery is profound, but I am talking about Christ and the church"

(Eph. 5:31–32). Paul was giving instructions to married couples regarding their duties and gender-specific responsibilities in marriage, and he quotes Genesis as he did to the Corinthians, pointing to the one flesh union fortified by sex. When I first read these verses as a young believer, the juxtaposition of marriage with Christ and the church confused me. I decided to ask a pastor to help make sense of what I believed was a strong and random shift in the flow of the letter, and he told me, "It isn't random at all; that pivot isn't actually a pivot. To understand Christ and the church, you need to understand marriage, and to understand marriage, you need to understand Christ and the church." When God made Adam and Eve, the gospel story was already in play, and their union would help us understand the good news.

So, what Paul is telling us is that the one flesh union of a husband and a wife is the visible picture of the invisible, spiritual reality of Christ and the church. By going back to Genesis, Paul followed Jesus' example in teaching on marriage. When Jesus was asked about divorce, he simply appealed to the untarnished, pre-fall garden of Eden. "'Haven't you read,' he replied, 'that he who created them in the beginning made them male and female, and he also said, "For this reason a man will leave his father and mother and be joined to his wife, and the two will become one flesh"? So they are no longer two, but one flesh. Therefore, what God has joined together, let no one separate'" (Matt. 19:4–6). While our union with Christ is eternal, the marriage union in this life nonetheless has an earthly permanence and is not to be broken.

"Don't you know that anyone joined to a prostitute is one body with her? For Scripture says, 'The two will become one flesh'" (1 Cor. 6:16). Paul is using the context of the actions at the Corinthian temple to communicate that sex is never "just sex." God's Word makes it clear that He cares for us enough to call us to flee from doing permanent things in temporary relationships. Permanence is to be found exclusively in marriage, where what God has joined together should not be separated.

Purity culture correctly understood that departing from God's design for sex leads to brokenness. The movement was right to make a big deal about the consequences of embracing the mindset of the world regarding sex. But what I have not heard from those who claim the name of Christ yet tremble at the mention of purity culture is an actual alternative. There is criticism, there are cries of legalism, and there are stories of the damage done by the movement, but what then are we to do? The best answer you might get is a call for nuance. Certainly, there are times where nuance is the best answer for complicated matters, but what the Bible says about sex is not one of those examples. Being upset or embarrassed about one's evangelical upbringing does not change the fact that God has a design. Extrabiblical measures championed by purity culture and evolving into legalism do not change the fact that God has a design. There is a thread from Genesis, through the Ten Commandments, to Jesus, and to Paul that points to a design that existed before the Fall. When we push back against biblical sexual ethics, we are embracing a post-fall understanding of sex, where the only remaining value is consent. A disdain for purity culture without a commitment to biblical sexual ethics will not shine the light of God's glory to a sexually broken world.

SEX IS LIKE FIRE. BARRIERS MATTER.

Purity culture often talked about sex in a manner that suggested it was a bad thing and should be feared. This is a fair critique. In God's design, nothing could be further from the truth. Sex is a beautiful, powerful thing that must be handled responsibly. Let me give an analogy. I'm from Florida, so having a fire burning in the fireplace is uncommon. But on the few nights a year we actually use our fireplace, our home has all the good feelings of Christmas, warmth, and nostalgia. Bring on the hot apple cider and the Hallmark Christmas movies—we have a fire burning! Fire in the fireplace is a wonderful thing. But if that fire escapes the fireplace and spreads even two feet and reaches the living room rug, this would be a terrible thing. We would rush to put it out so it wouldn't spread. This would definitely put a damper on our Hallmark movie. Fire itself isn't the issue, but the location of the fire makes a drastic difference. Put on your fuzzy socks if there is fire in the fireplace; frantically grab the fire extinguisher if there is fire on the rug. Fire in a fireplace is great, fire on the rug is not great. (That's why a loving parent would teach their kids how to properly behave around fire.)

Sex itself isn't the problem. It is sex outside of God's design that is the problem, like fire on a rug instead of in the fireplace. Sex isn't evil, but taken outside its prescribed barriers, it can be incredibly destructive. When sex is presented as something bad, when God is thought of as some sort of killjoy, we are implying something that is inconsistent with His creative power and design. (Who do you think invented sex? Hint: it's not people from the 1960s.) We should instead take our cue from the writer of Hebrews, who said, "Marriage is to be honored by all and the marriage bed kept undefiled, because God will judge the sexually immoral and adulterers" (13:4). Sex should be held in high esteem in the same way one would look out at a mountain range and marvel at what God has designed and created. Moreover, Hebrews tells us what the opposite looks like—sexual immorality and adultery. It's never just sex.

I often tell our congregation:

Sex is not for "in love" people.
Sex is not for mature people.
Sex is not for careful people.
Sex is for married people.

PURITY CULTURE & FALSE ADVERTISING

Another misstep of purity culture is assuming that sex within marriage is a sexual utopia. Walking into marriage believing this can lead to confusion, frustration, and feeling like something is wrong with you if sex doesn't seem perfect immediately. The fire in the fireplace needs tending and care; building a good fire takes time. Sex can be imperfect for those who remained virgins until their wedding night and for those who didn't. There is healing for some and learning for others. The point is that marriage is the only proper relationship in which those aspects of a sexual relationship should be experienced. From repairing brokenness to learning the complexities of the human body, marriage is the forum that God provided.

In a world that has departed from God's design for sex (and has celebrated that departure and sought to indoctrinate the next generation in it), the societal consequences of sexual sin will continue to be a reality in our lives. The anti-purity culture angst seems to want to pretend all is fine, but it is not. People are broken, and brokenness is the only logical outcome of departing Eden and God's design. When we have, as Paul stated, sinned "against our own bodies," the way forward is not to get upset with those who continue to contend for God's design but rather to believe the gospel and embrace the great alternative that Paul reveals: "But anyone joined to the Lord is one spirit with him" (1 Cor. 6:17).

The only way to healing is in Christ. While our union with Christ restores our relationship with God instantly and for eternity, the long trail back to Eden begins with individual steps of obedience. Our sanctification includes pursuing God's design for sex, and, by His grace, He allows those who have sinned to recover His purposes and begin living according to His design. For those who have either sinned or been sinned against by others, have hope.

My prayer is that those who have been corrupted by sin and carried into darkness will believe that Jesus came to redeem, restore, and make new. Jesus came to bring life and light that shines in the darkest places. The path back to Eden is paved in Christ.

SECTION

PASSING THROUGH:
Living as Exiles
in a Sex-Crazed World

Now that we have briefly covered the purity culture our current generation is rejecting, as well as the counter swing to a worldly ideology, I'd like to home in on that hallowed narrow gate that points to God's design. For the next few chapters, we will examine various areas in which many Christians need to recover proper footing, such as views on dating, singleness, homosexuality, and pornography. But a primary thread connecting these is an understanding that we are exiles in this world. We are just passing through. Our behaviors are not meant to mirror (or even make sense to) those of the world.

Apart from going out of state for college, I have lived in Florida my entire life. Generally, you have three different options for scenery in our state: beaches, swampland, or a whole lot of trees. One summer, my wife and I went to northern Wyoming for a vacation. We stayed close to Yellowstone National Park and enjoyed being in one of the most beautiful states and settings in America. We saw wildlife and terrain that were foreign to us, like bison and actual mountains. Being out in the American West, I was really tempted to buy a cowboy hat and some boots, which were seemingly available in every store and worn by all the locals. But I am not a cowboy, I am a Floridian, and Western garb wasn't practical for my real life or where I was going: home.

Followers of Christ are citizens of a different world—a spiritual one, a world that is being prepared for the church. According to the author of Hebrews, the common theme of believers who lived by faith in God's promises was their desire for a better place—a heavenly one (Heb. 11:16). Peter reminded the church that they were "strangers and exiles" (1 Peter 2:11), and Paul pointed the Philippian believers to their citizenship in heaven (Phil. 3:20). Like I felt as a Floridian visiting Wyoming, Christians should feel like visitors as they sojourn through this life, as if it is a foreign world. Scripture makes clear that the people of God should not resemble the world because they are a distinct nation living under God's reign. Due to our sinful nature, there are times when believers lose sight of their status as people of another kingdom and begin to blend into this world through sinful actions. For those who genuinely know the Lord, however, there is repentance and a desire to no longer be conformed to the patterns of the world (Rom. 12:2). If you have fallen into sin or have never heard biblical teaching on some of the forthcoming topics, please know that in Christ there is full forgiveness, cleansing, newness of life, and community.

For many twenty-first century American Christians, a prevalent area of blending with the world is the realm of sex, dating, and relationships. Biblical teaching regarding sexual ethics has always stood at odds with the world, and, frankly, there are professing Christians who are not interested in being at odds anymore. Today, many Christians would rather be on the "right side" of issues in the world's eyes. The Bible allows for a societally acceptable stance on poverty and racial reconciliation, but many Christians seem embarrassed by the clear sexual ethics the Bible calls them to pursue under the lordship of Christ. The world applauds caring about the poor but accuses the church of oppressive, out-of-date extremism when it comes to what the Bible says about sexuality. In a Twitter thread on the connection between biblical views of justice and sexual purity, Tim Keller wrote that the early church was marked by a deep concern for the poor and for racial equality, and at the same time, it taught that sex was only for the mutually self-giving and life-long covenant of marriage.[1] Keller remarked that these two are a "whole cloth united by the principle of self-sacrifice, of 'losing one's self to find one's self.'"[2] In Christ, we can understand how the Bible's teaching on sex is consistent with its broader calls to self-sacrifice, whereas the world may not have a legitimate model for that.

There are others who (rather than being embarrassed) simply do not want to be bothered by what the Bible says about sex, who see God as a type of prude or view biblical sexual ethics as something reserved for legalists. Perhaps they see it as an inconvenience for religious beliefs to interfere with such personal life choices. As a result, too many professing Christians today identify more with Carrie Bradshaw from Sex in the City than with the True Love Waits card of another era. The pendulum has swung to a "if you can't beat 'em, join 'em" mentality.

The sexual ethics of the world should feel like a foreign land to followers of Jesus, but I see many falling into the norms of a secular society while still claiming Christian faith and identity. The next few chapters will dive into seven primary lies that Christians may believe as they sojourn through this life on earth.

LIE NO. 1:
"Sex is Expected"

To enter a dating relationship in our day is the equivalent of agreeing to only sleep with each other for the period during which the couple remains in the relationship. What was once the first kiss is now sleeping together. This is especially prevalent on college campuses, where "hookup culture" is a normal part of the experience for many. The American Psychological Association has even written a definition for "hookup" as "a type of sexual encounter in which the participants have no expectation of continuing or developing their relationship beyond the sexual encounter."[1] In a reflection upon the hookup culture of her college experience, a female student wrote, "With time, inevitably, came attachment. And with attachment came shame, anxiety, and emptiness. My girlfriends and I were top students, scientists, artists, and leaders. We could advocate for anything—except for our own bodies. We won accolades from our professors, but the men we were sleeping with wouldn't even eat breakfast with us the next morning. What's worse, we really thought of the situation in those terms: 'He didn't ask to grab breakfast, so I walked home.'"[2]

I hate assuming the worst, but after being in pastoral ministry for a significant amount of time surrounded by nominal Christianity and many public university students, I can tell you that it is rare for a dating couple to have anything less than a physical relationship. They might not be literally having sex, but usually some level of foreplay is taking place. One reason I can assert this is because I am regularly told this by couples who are living in that reality in their relationships. In a type of faux commitment where much of married life is acted out by being together constantly, when a couple exchanges deep emotions and passionate kisses, the temptation is almost unbearable.

To guard against sexual temptation, the critical factor for a Christian should be certainty that the person he or she is dating is a Christian of strong convictions. This does not guarantee sexual purity, but it starts you off wisely in a relationship with someone who is not of this world and is striving to follow Christ. When a Christian begins dating an unbeliever, he or she is likely walking into a world where sex is expected. This should not be a surprise. Sometimes the initial rhetoric is that the unbeliever "respects" the other person's beliefs and isn't going to pressure anything, but that usually doesn't last long. I also wonder if Christians who are dating unbelievers realize what is communicated by that relationship: that faith is not important to them in finding a future spouse. Being attracted to another person, admiring a great personality, feeling some sort of chemistry—those are apparently more important than faith. Yes, there are stories of people being led to Christ through this practice (often called "missionary dating"), but this merely shows that God is bigger than our bad decisions and misplaced priorities. Not to mention that if sex is part of a missionary dating relationship that results in a conversion to Christianity, my concern would be that the individual was won to something other than Christ. Perhaps he or she now attends church with the girlfriend or boyfriend's family, but is that person truly following Christ? Furthermore, if the Christian in the relationship is living in sin, why would we think genuine conversion is taking place without repentance?

These are not hypothetical situations; they are commonplace among Christians who are more concerned with being in a relationship than with what God says about relationships. As a result, the sexual ethics of the Bible become an inconvenience rather than something to be pursued. I am hard pressed to find any reason to blame purity culture for the sad reality that Christians are being absorbed into the world's expectation of sex. If anything, we are seeing an over-correction from purity culture encouraged by an absence of biblical teaching on sex from the pulpit. Sermons about relationships often tiptoe around the matter, focusing on how to find Mr. Right or how to have a good marriage rather than on how to remain faithful in a world that sees sex as an expectation and not as a gift from God for the lifelong covenant of marriage. Dating an unbeliever and entering a relationship where sex is expected are often the initial steps of compromise that I see a Christians taking on the road to disappearing from Christian community and, ultimately, the faith altogether.

The sequence usually goes like this:

A Christian man or woman who hasn't dated much starts to get attention from someone he or she finds attractive, whom he or she met outside of a church community (most commonly at school, work, or in a social setting). The two start to flirt and eventually make plans to get together outside of work or wherever they met. All of this so far is based on physical attraction and is usually void of any conversation about faith. Each person has no idea whether the other is a Christian.

A date takes place and is very enjoyable. Mutual attraction

creates a rush, a sense of euphoria, and they feel like something exciting is beginning.

As more dates occur, all the aspects of a relationship have begun. Increased time spent together eventually leads to a physical relationship. However small the compromise begins, it usually and persistently grows to places the Christian would have never intended. But he or she likes the attention and the feeling of being desired, wanted, and pursued. There are also feelings of guilt, but no one in the Christian community knows about the relationship for now.

Eventually, the Christian's community of friends from church finds out about the relationship. The friends are excited but ask about the new love interest's faith. By this point, there is no denying that the significant other isn't following Jesus or is disinterested in the faith altogether. It is most likely that he or she merely "respects" the beliefs of the Christian person, seeing that they have presented virtually no hindrance to the relationship. Knowing this, the Christian pivots the conversation away from faith to instead focus on how great and "supportive" the boyfriend or girlfriend is—maybe he or she is even open to attending church sometime.

The friends push back with concern, and this quickly escalates to the person in the relationship feeling that their friends are being judgmental, legalistic, and unfair. Or, even worse, they make claims such as "you don't want me to be happy" or "you're just jealous because you haven't found someone."

Ultimately, the person in the unsanctioned relationship pulls away completely from his or her friend group, claiming that the church has become judgmental, convinced that he or she has a righteous cause to continue in this relationship as some sort of missionary. Maybe the person will slip in the back row where he or she can be anonymous or attend a different church with the significant other that would never preach on sexual ethics or make a big deal about a believer dating an unbeliever. Eventually they stop going to church at all and the unbeliever's friends become the believer's new friends, leaving him or her without any Christian community.

Oh, and they live together.

This sequence functions like a script because it is par for the course. As a pastor, one of the primary reasons I see people walk away from church community is because they have entered a relationship that is forbidden or unwise. This may be a dating relationship, an extramarital affair, or a homosexual relationship, but sexual relationships are almost always the reason. When we combine our natural yearning for a relationship with a world where sex is expected, it's almost guaranteed that the relationship will become sexual or that the Christian's convictions will irritate the other person and the couple will break up. I am not trying to villainize unbelievers. I'm also not claiming that sex is inevitable in a dating relationship. Rather, I am stating that a believer is most vulnerable when two completely different sets of convictions regarding sex come together. Someone's convictions are going to run that relationship. While the apostle Paul's words to the Corinthian church regarding being "unequally yoked" are not necessarily in the context of a dating relationship, the principle absolutely applies in this scenario: "Do not be yoked together with those who do not believe. For what partnership is there between righteousness and lawlessness? Or what fellowship does light have with darkness? What agreement does Christ have with Belial? Or what does a believer have in common with an unbeliever?" (2 Cor. 6:14–15).

What does a believer have in common with an unbeliever? Similar hobbies and personalities that "gel" equate to little in common at all without Christ. For a Christian dating couple who share convictions from the Scriptures, sex may be a temptation, but it should never be an expectation. Therefore, since dating is the typical avenue to engagement and marriage, Christian individuals and communities must be clear about where Scripture draws lines in terms of sexual ethics. Battling sexual temptation with a fellow believer and seeking godly help in doing so is a far cry from starting a relationship in secret with someone who has a completely different set of beliefs regarding sex. Single Christians need to be particular about who is an acceptable dating partner.

One thing that the True Love Waits generation should be thankful for is that we were discipled in an era when it was engrained in us that sex in a dating relationship was unacceptable in the eyes of God. This doesn't mean we were immune from temptation—we entered dating relationships full of hormones and puppy love. But sex was not an expectation because we were taught to understand that sex was not for dating people, in-love people, or committed people, but for married people. Christians must be both unashamed of God's Word and unhindered by angst toward purity culture so we don't fail to make disciples who are fully aware of what God has said and fully equipped to walk in it.

5

LIE NO. 2:
"Marriage is a Capstone, Not a Cornerstone"[1]

Traditionally, the cornerstone of a building is a solid, foundational piece commemorating the importance or significance of the structure.[2] Once the building is completed, a capstone is a piece placed on the top of an exterior wall. In short, the building is built *from* the cornerstone and is *finalized with* a capstone. As a church in a large university context, we regularly celebrate students from our congregation getting engaged, often in their junior or senior year of college. A major component of our church culture is encouraging people to pursue marriage in their dating relationships rather than date for years. While we certainly don't flippantly suggest that every couple just getting to know each other should get married a month later, our leadership team's commitment to preaching God's design creates a culture where our members don't put off marriage as something to think about down the road but rather see it as something from which to build their lives. In other words, marriage at our church is viewed as a cornerstone of life, not something you might think about eventually or tack on to whatever else you pursued first.

The secular view of marriage in our day is the exact opposite: to the world, marriage is a capstone, not a cornerstone. Once you finish your master's degree, travel, save money, and maybe even buy a house or spend time living in your dream city, then, sure—if you really want to—get married. We are seeing a generation of well-meaning Christians buy into this life plan. I'm not talking about people for whom singleness is a gift and who intentionally live a single life to God's glory. I'm talking about people who have every intention of getting married, just not before they do everything they think is really important first.

This does not mean Christians can't pursue advanced degrees, travel the world, or get their footing in a career. When I was a junior in college, my (now) wife Krissie and I began dating, and I wanted to get married as soon as we graduated. Following what I thought was conventional wisdom, I figured I needed to be saving money in order to get married. That was not the easiest endeavor since I was going to school full-time and working part-time as a waiter to pay for basic things like gas and food. Thankfully, because of my parents, I wasn't in need, but the idea of saving money for marriage seemed laughable. One day after class, I approached my biblical counseling professor for advice. I had just one question: "How much money do you need to save up before you get married?" I was convinced there was a universal total sum out there that I hadn't been told about yet.

My professor listened to my question, thought over it for a couple seconds, and said, "One month's living expenses would probably be helpful."

Wait, what about the magic number?

Didn't I need $10,000, or maybe even $50,000, in the bank? I thought she was messing with me, so I laughed a little in response. Detecting I wasn't convinced, she asked, "Can you pay for your rent now?" I nodded my head. "Then you're fine, just make sure you can eat and pay your car insurance." Well, okay, then! I could figure that out. Krissie had been working all through college too, so I might have even guessed we could pay double rent! I saved up for her engagement ring and made sure we had at least one month's living expenses. We even had some extra money for fun thanks to wedding gifts. Engaged at 21 and 22, married at 22 and 23.

Getting married young is often frowned upon today, especially by those outside of religious communities. While being twenty-two years old a few generations ago meant you were invading the beaches of Normandy, today a twenty-two-year-old is classified as a kid. The assumption seems to be that you will miss out on life by getting married young, as if there is some sort of pre-marriage bucket list you must complete first. As a result, marriage is viewed as a capstone—as icing on the cake of whatever else your life becomes. My wife and I were under the conviction from Scripture that marriage and family as designed by God are things to build our lives from, together, rather than things to get to eventually if we had time. If we had viewed marriage as a capstone, I guess we would have kept dating for years, increasingly prone to sexual temptation, all in the name of saving money, earning another degree, or backpacking Europe. Paul told the Corinthian Christians that if they did not have self-control, they should marry, since it is better to marry than to burn with desire (1 Cor. 7:9). We weren't designed to pursue any type of intense intimacy without the marriage covenant in place. Paul isn't saying you should get married only because you want to have sex, but if you want to have sex, you need to get married.

Sadly, parents can be one of the biggest obstacles to people getting married at an age our culture views as young. There is a stigma attached to not being established in life before marriage. Nobody is actually defining what it means to be "established," but getting married young is now taboo, and parents may feel embarrassed or insecure when the response of friends to their son or daughter's engagement is, "Oh, wow, so young."

Parents may also object for financial reasons, but the ramifications of this are far from insignificant. Parents insisting that their sons or daughters delay marriage until they accumulate resources suggests that financial instability is a bigger concern than sexual immorality. In my context, I see this regularly from Christian families. To be fair, I don't think they know what is communicated by their actions. Do Christians actually believe that sexual immorality is not as big of a deal as having to live frugally for the first few years of marriage? I highly doubt it, but the world's wisdom is so insidious that parents have not only been influenced by the idea of marriage as a capstone but are now unknowingly promoting it to their kids.

A quick aside: It is possible that parents would say their objections are not financial or societal. Instead, they may question the judgment of their son or daughter who wants to get married because they are worried that he or she doesn't understand the weight of the commitment or might not be drawn to the same person past his or her late teens and early twenties. And there's merit to these concerns. My kids aren't yet marriage age, so I'm sure I'll wrestle with this. But those same parents should also have already been instructing their kids on the seriousness of marriage and modeling commitment throughout and despite changing life circumstances.

When I teach on the subject of marriage, I have often said to our congregation and college students: "How do I know Krissie is the one for me? I married her." God is committed to the marriage relationship. If you're married, that's the person He wants you to be with.

One young man in our church had a strong conflict with his parents regarding whether he had to finish college before he got married. While it isn't necessarily unreasonable for parents to ask their son to complete his undergraduate degree before getting married, he and his girlfriend (now wife) had been dating for quite some time, and there was nothing keeping them from getting married other than a college graduation. Reflecting on that conflict with his parents, he told me he truly believed that they would have been less outraged if he and his girlfriend had decided to live together as an unmarried couple than they would be about their getting married before his graduation. His parents are professing Christians. In a world where marriage is a capstone rather than a cornerstone, this story is not an outlier. Perhaps parents of young adults forget how they started out themselves, which likely included marrying young (as was common practice in earlier generations). But marrying later (or with money in the bank) still can't shield a grown son or daughter from the struggles that marriage brings. The view of marriage as a cornerstone accepts the challenges that come with two sinners building their lives together and sees trials as part of the process of growing in Christ as husband and wife.

The idea of financial struggle is quite subjective, too. Living in a small apartment and being unable to buy the latest smartphone

may seem like a tragedy for parents who raised their kids in afflu-
ence, but how quick are those parents to forget that they probably
didn't live like fifty-five-year-olds when they were twenty-two and
first married? If you wait to get married until you can afford whatever, whenever, marriage will inevitably become a capstone while
serious dating relationships will most likely remain a part of life.
This can set people up for life outside of God's design for intimate
relationships. In addition, the local church can and should serve
as a haven for new couples, offering the sort of familial and sacrificial community that would allow Christians to enter marriage
without having to worry about being financially adrift in the face
of unforeseen needs.

I remember finally getting the courage to have "the talk" with
my now father-in-law. When you ask a man for permission to
marry his daughter, usually he asks you, "How do you plan to
support my daughter?" That's what I was expecting to hear, and I
was dreading the question because I had no real answer. Our plan
after our wedding was to head to seminary, where I would be a
full-time graduate student and Krissie would be the one working.
My answer to the famous question would have been, "My plan
to support your daughter is actually that she is going to support
me!" I will forever be grateful that my father-in-law never asked
the question. He simply gave his support and blessing. Finances
weren't his concern. He knew we were committed to Christ and
to each other and wanted to be married, and he gave his support.

At the time I didn't realize how countercultural my father-in-
law was being. But looking back, I now realize he saw marriage as
a cornerstone, and not just in theory—he lived it out and meant
it for his daughter as well. Krissie and I got married and moved
to our small seminary apartment. It was dated, stale, and certainly
not a dream home. We paid our bills thanks to my wife's job as a
secretary and my shifts as a museum tour guide between seminary

classes. Our parents let us have the cars we had been driving, and my parents graciously paid for my seminary classes. My wife and I look back to our seminary apartment days with great joy. True, we didn't get to eat at restaurants as much as we would have liked, and we bought our couch at a garage sale and had the most basic cable package imaginable. But we were together as husband and wife, building our lives from the cornerstone of the marriage covenant. Visiting our parents for holidays felt like going to five-star hotels compared to where we were living, but what made it best was that we got to go together—not in a pretend marriage called dating, with sexual temptation hovering over us regularly, but as two people committed to one another, living in God's design.

At the church where I serve as a pastor, college students regularly get engaged and married shortly after graduation. Occasionally, we see students get married while still in school earning their undergraduate degrees. The members in our church who serve as premarital counselors certainly make sure the young couples are aware of the challenges of getting married while still in college, but they celebrate the decision if both parties are serious about the commitment. I passionately believe that Christians cannot be on a crusade against purity culture while simultaneously being against getting married young. This is not because purity culture was without serious flaws but rather because opposing marriage removes the primary viable option. If the call of Scripture is sexual purity, and if a Christian wants to get married, why would other Christians block that road? Why is it that one can contend for the truth of the resurrection of Christ or the call to love one's neighbor but flinch at a couple pursuing God's clear design for marriage and sexuality, who are convicted to live in step with Paul's call to the Corinthians to marry rather than commit sexual immorality? As churches have begun to promote an emphasis on self-realization and pursuit of things that may delay marriage (or even fail to promote marriage as a legitimate option for young adults), we're seeing a trend of professing Christians normalizing long-term singleness without the expectation of celibacy. But the Bible has no exemption clauses for people who are dating. If marriage is not a reality for a Christian, sexual purity is still expected and commanded.

When we break God's design, we should expect brokenness, not bliss.

This is not because God has rules for the sake of rules, though He certainly has that right, but because God cares for His own glory and for His image bearers. Imagine a world where, besides the initial surprise, a woman doesn't have to be terrified when a pregnancy test is positive. Think of a world where, after you give yourself to another person sexually, there isn't any anxiety that he or she might not acknowledge you in public. There is freedom when a couple commits to practicing sex in the context of a lifelong covenant relationship that God designed (called marriage), in which the husband commits to love his wife as Christ loved the church and the wife to respect her husband.

When we break God's design, we should expect brokenness, not bliss. But living by God's design isn't wishful thinking, it is absolutely possible! The world's wisdom regarding marriage is to save money, date lots of people, check lots of items off your bucket list, and then, if you're ready to settle down, give marriage a shot. Thankfully, God tells us exactly His will for His people. Paul gives us an incredibly helpful insight into the mind of God: "For this is God's will, your sanctification" (1 Thess. 4:3). Talk about being as clear as possible! People have searched, wrestled, tossed and turned at night, and even done pilgrimages in order to find God's will, and here Paul puts it right in front of us. He says God's will is our sanctification, our growing in holiness. Paul, writing under the inspiration of the Holy Spirit, then gives Christians a specific example of what sanctification looks like: "that you keep away from sexual immorality" (v. 3). It doesn't get any clearer than that. God's will is our sanctification, our sexual purity. Paul goes a step further in describing what that looks like and then drives home the big point, "that each of you knows how to control his own body in holiness and honor, not with lustful passions, like the Gentiles, who don't know God" (vv. 4–5). God expects His people, both married and unmarried, to control their bodies when it comes to sexual temptation. To refuse to do so is to resemble people who do not know God. We are least like the world when we submit our bodies to the One they belong to in the first place: God Himself. When we avoid sexual immorality, we are carrying out God's will for us. God instructs us to "flee sexual immorality" (1 Cor. 6:18), not flirt with it, get as close to the line as possible, or even see how resistant we can be in the moment. Viewing marriage as a capstone and dating in the meantime, doesn't align with the wisdom of God but with that of the world. First John says that "the world with its lust is passing away, but the one who does the will of God remains forever" (2:17).

Marriage on the other hand has certainly not passed away. Let's look at this thread throughout Scripture:

The account of Creation in Genesis 2:18–25:

> Then the LORD God said, "It is not good for the man to be alone. I will make a helper corresponding to him." The LORD God formed out of the ground every wild animal and every bird of the sky, and brought each to the man to see what he would call it. And whatever the man called a living creature, that was its name. The man gave names to all the livestock, to the birds of the sky, and to every wild animal; but for the man no helper was found corresponding to him. So the LORD God

caused a deep sleep to come over the man, and he slept. God took one of his ribs and closed the flesh at that place. Then the LORD God made the rib he had taken from the man into a woman and brought her to the man. And the man said:

> This one, at last, is bone of my bone
> and flesh of my flesh;
> this one will be called "woman,"
> for she was taken from man.

This is why a man leaves his father and mother and bonds with his wife, and they become one flesh. Both the man and his wife were naked, yet felt no shame.

Jesus, in Matthew 19:4–6: "'Haven't you read,' he replied, 'that he who created them in the beginning made them male and female, and he also said, "For this reason a man will leave his father and mother and be joined to his wife, and the two will become one flesh"? So they are no longer two, but one flesh. Therefore, what God has joined together, let no one separate.'"

Paul, writing to the Ephesians in approximately AD 62: "For this reason a man will leave his father and mother and be joined to his wife, and the two will become one flesh" (5:31).

The writer of Hebrews: "Marriage is to be honored by all and the marriage bed kept undefiled, because God will judge the sexually immoral and adulterers" (13:4).

Beginning in Genesis and continuing throughout the Bible, marriage is elevated as the model. Singleness is great, and marriage is great. But a sort of loose, flexible partnering is not. God created marriage to be a cornerstone. Let us live out His will regarding our sanctification by fleeing from sexual immorality until we are ready to pursue a relationship that leads to marriage.

6

LIE NO. 3:
"Porn is the Norm"

Sports Illustrated magazine was a staple for sports fans in the pre-internet world, myself included. Once a week, the magazine would be delivered to fans eager to look at photos and commentary on the previous week in sports. One of the great honors in sports during this era was to appear on the cover of the magazine. I remember running out to check the mailbox as a kid to see if the latest issue had come, and I would usually try to guess which athlete or team would be on the cover based on all that had happened in the world of sports that week. I would grab the magazine out of the mailbox, run to my room, and soak up every page.

But there was one week each year that I wasn't allowed to immerse myself in the legendary magazine, and that was when the annual "Swimsuit Edition" would come in the mail. My dad would take the magazine out of my hands and throw it away. He didn't want his eleven-year-old son flipping through an issue completely devoted to showcasing women in skimpy bathing suits. I thought he was being a killjoy at the time, but as I look back, I'm grateful for my dad protecting my eyes and mind from something I did not need to be exposed to—the bodies of women who were not my wife. My dad kept me from soft pornography.

While the swimsuit issue of *Sports Illustrated* didn't show nudity at the time, it was the closest thing to pictures of naked women many boys my age could get, unless you had a friend with a rebellious older brother who bought *Playboy* magazines from behind the counter at a gas station. However, while pornography was not necessarily easy to access, "sex as entertainment" and a growing exploitation and celebration of sex were taking over TV sitcoms and music videos on MTV. Dramatic TV series targeted at younger audiences portrayed characters in high school having sex for the first time, and the full incorporation of sex into entertainment was no longer reserved for X-rated movie theaters in a sketchy part of town. Today, sex scenes in movies and TV series are normal and seemingly inescapable. This is significant, because only rarely have I met someone who began his or her viewing of pornography with an X-rated movie directly from the pornography industry. Pornography viewing also rarely starts with material from the Hugh Hefner or Larry Flynt realm. It usually starts with simple expressions of lust. A scene from a mainstream movie, an Instagram post from a beach trip, or a targeted ad by some lifestyle blog or clothing company. It usually starts out "small." And now, people don't even have to look for lewd or sexualized content to be inundated with it.

"The first part of the word pornography, 'porné,' means immorality and the second part, 'graph' means to write, draw, or portray. Pornography is about picturing, imagining, and fantasizing about immorality."[1] We deceive ourselves by thinking we can rationalize sexual sin if we are not engaging in physical actions with another person, but Jesus spoke to the seriousness of fantasizing immorality when He said, "You have heard that it was said, 'Do not commit adultery.' But I tell you, everyone who looks at a woman lustfully has already committed adultery with her in his heart" (Matt. 5:27–28). God sees into our hearts and minds even if others cannot.

The world is self-contradictory on this issue too, because while it celebrates almost any expression of sex, it is not hard to find non-Christian people who have issue with the pornography industry. It is common knowledge that it fuels human trafficking and preys on vulnerable people. The fact that pornography remains a billion-dollar industry shows the extent of brokenness in our world and the prevalence of predatory behavior with zero regard for the well-being of others. I don't need to convince readers of this book about the dangers and evils of pornography. Christians I counsel who are battling pornography addiction are well aware of what it can do to someone's mind and habits and know the tragic effects it can have on relationships and marriages. But my fear is that in this heightened anti-purity culture moment in which the church finds itself, wishing to avoid being labelled as fundamentalists or "that kind of Christian," many are becoming passive in how they view entertainment, and others push back against the idea of modesty. I would like to address entertainment and modesty here, as they impact all of us, not just those who have a weakness for lust or pornography.

ENTERTAINMENT: A COVENANT WITH MY EYES

As I think back to my dad not allowing me to have the swimsuit issue of *Sports Illustrated*, I miss the time when protecting your kids from temptation was viewed as loving. Today, especially on social media, just mentioning what one should not see immediately results in others leaping to the conclusion that you are guilty of objectification. These quick, accusatory reactions are also coming from Christians, many of whom are ready to label you an oppressor, misogynist, or a sexual objectifier of your sisters in Christ. Due to a lack of sober-minded conversation among Christians, there is now great difficulty in navigating a world where porn is the norm, especially in defining exactly what is inappropriate. Christians have become desensitized to the reality of pornography. Some have had a chip on their shoulders concerning entertainment, feeling that Christian art and entertainment lag behind the quality of what is being produced by the secular world. As a result, often in the spirit of showing they are not lame or sheltered, many have a desire to embrace whatever film or TV series the surrounding society is watching.

A few years ago, Kevin DeYoung wrote about his confusion over why Christians were enthralled with the hit series *Game of Thrones*, asking, "Does anyone really think that when Jesus warned against looking at a woman lustfully (Matt. 5:27), or when Paul told us to avoid every hint of sexual immorality and not even to speak of the things the world does in secret (Eph. 5:3–12), that somehow this meant, go ahead and watch naked men and women have (or pretend to have) sex?"[2] When I first read Kevin's brief article back in 2017, in the height of the show's popularity, I immediately thought, "Oh, he stepped in a hornet's nest, people are going to lose their minds," and—on cue—Christians pushed back. DeYoung wrote a follow-up post sharing the objections he received from professing Christians who were upset or disagreed with his convictions. One of the objections he listed was one to be expected: "Stop judging and shaming!"[3] The article did not belittle anyone or leave people without hope; it simply asked how viewing such a show was wise or permissible for anyone claiming to follow Jesus Christ. This is where we are in this cultural moment. Speak directly about sexual immorality, including that of the mind, and you are out of bounds. And this is to other Christians! Another objection was that "most shows have good and bad elements," suggesting that the story and artistry outweigh the explicit scenes.[4] This reminds me of the jokes people made when I was growing up about only reading *Playboy* for the articles or going to Hooters because of the chicken wings.

DeYoung concludes his piece by stating that at the "heart of the matter" is "an implicit assumption; namely, that immersing ourselves in sensual entertainment is somehow a gray area of Christian liberty."[5] Is it legalism and shaming now to simply say that this matter is clear in the Scriptures? Apparently so, given our societal reaction toward the memory of purity culture. If you can find "a single, compelling argument for the legitimacy of Christians viewing graphic sex scenes,"[6] you have accomplished something no theologian before you has, and you should join the next Bigfoot expedition. DeYoung asks:

> Does anyone actually think the apostle Paul (or any other apostle, or Jesus for that matter) would have been cool with the sensuality prevalent in *Game of Thrones* (and so much of our entertainment)? We are not talking about marble statues or a Holocaust documentary or a physician examining a patient. We are talking about two naked people doing in front of us what naked people do together. Take the medium of television out of it. Would you go into a private room and look through a peep hole to watch this? Would anyone think that's the sort of thing we can give thanks for? Or the sort of thing mature Christians do?[7]

One can feel his tone range from puzzlement to frustration. Christians are not supposed to be of this world, and I can't help but fear what is in store in the future thought lives of those who can justify sitting through sexual scenes on film or TV unbothered. I once had a conversation with an individual who was unable to have

sex with his wife due to the online pornography world into which
he had fully immersed himself. The sexual scenes he watched as frequently as daily had desensitized his mind and body. The fantasy
images of his online world became normal in his mind, and this
prohibited him from being able to engage sexually with his wife.
This was a tragedy and had a tremendous effect on their marriage.
But I mention his story because his trail down the dark road of pornography began not with intense X-rated scenes on his computer
but with ads depicting women in revealing clothing that appeared
on his social media feeds. Once those became a fixation of his mind,
he desired more, and the road continued to a genre of pornography
that cannot be explained except as complete darkness and filth.

When I was in high school, one of my youth leaders had the
boys in our Bible study group memorize a verse that I am thankful to still remember today. In my times of weakness and vulnerability regarding lust, it still rings in my mind. It is Job 31:1: "I
have made a covenant with my eyes. How then could I look at
a young woman?" This is such an easy verse to memorize, and it
lines up with the Psalmist's words, "I have treasured your word in
my heart so that I may not sin against you" (Ps. 119:11).

Speaking to an audience eons before the internet, Jesus made
His stance on lust truly clear by using hyperbole. "If your right
eye causes you to sin, gouge it out and throw it away. For it is better that you lose one of the parts of your body than for your whole
body to be thrown into hell. And if your right hand causes you to
sin, cut it off and throw it away. For it is better that you lose one of
the parts of your body than for your whole body to go into hell"
(Matt. 5:29–30). What a statement. While Jesus is not suggesting
that Christians self-mutilate if they give in to lust, He is expecting us to be willing to take drastic measures to pursue holiness.
We are not just trying to overcome lustful desires for the sake
of overcoming lustful desires. We also are not trying to win the

battle against lust primarily because we have families and want to be faithful spouses. We want to win the battle because we are followers of Jesus Christ. He is worthy of our lives, and He calls us to pursue a life of purity. It is God's will for His people to flee sexual immorality (1 Cor. 6:18). He cares for His own glory and desires that His people not wreck their lives with sexual addiction and broken relationships. As the redeemed people of God, we are called to "be imitators of God, as dearly loved children, and walk in love, as Christ also loved us and gave himself for us, a sacrificial and fragrant offering to God. But sexual immorality and any impurity or greed should not even be heard of among you, as is proper for saints" (Eph. 5:1–3). Sexual immorality and the call upon the children of God are at complete odds with each other. We are His possession. Our purpose for purity is Christ.

As I counsel men, I point them to the words of Christ that call believers to gouge out our eyes and cut off our hands if they cause us to sin, and I simply ask them what they are willing to eliminate from their lives to resist temptation. Are you willing to have the first world inconvenience of a phone without internet or data? Are you willing to cancel your Netflix account? Only have a computer in a shared location where your spouse or roommate has to log you in? Disconnect your internet? When I make suggestions like this, they're often laughed at as over-the-top and extreme or shrugged off as unrealistic. Yet I think of Jesus telling the rich young man to sell his belongings and follow Him (Matt. 19). We are told the man went away sad because he was wealthy. In other words, he was not willing to do what Jesus asked. And he missed out on Jesus.

I'm convinced that people must be willing to do whatever it takes to win the war against lust exhibited in pornography, and that seems to be what Jesus was commanding in His hyperbolic language. As outdated or inconvenient as it might be, it may be better to not have cable or internet at home. What may sound foolish to others, or even in your own mind, does not need to be complicated. Rather, you must answer the simple question, "Is it worth it?" Or, put more directly, which master is worth serving? Smartphones are hardly fifteen years old, and already it seems insane to suggest that someone go without one—that is how accustomed we've become to the things of this world. We say we follow Jesus, but not so much that it messes with our entertainment choices or conveniences. Is life with Christ worth doing whatever it takes to lay aside the sin that easily entangles us (Heb. 12), or are we at a point where it is legalistic to ask such a question?

MODESTY: WE EACH PLAY A ROLE

This conversation isn't just for people addicted to or tempted by pornography. It's for all of us. Every Christian must be willing to seriously weigh our actions and thoughts in our pursuit of Christ. I fear that the American church at large has become so afraid of being labelled oppressive or problematic that we can no longer approach any sort of sexual ethics conversation. Another area where this often plays out is talking about modesty. I'm not at all implying that a man's lust is a woman's fault. Not at all. But I am asserting that all believers are in submission to Christ and must heed His commands. So while some people need the Spirit's help to not look with lust, others may need the Spirit's help to not desire that attention. As a male, I am hesitant to even broach the topic, though I feel strongly that there is much to be said. So, I'll lean on the words of some women who have written on this topic.

In a brief and helpful piece on modesty, Megan Hill writes, "Christians decrying the legalism of purity culture recoil from teaching that would seek to lay out standards for dress and sexual conduct specifically aimed at women and not specifically named in Scripture. On the other hand, the unbelieving world throws off all limits for sexual self-expression and hates any attempt to correct someone's choices."[8] But in the church, this must not be so, for as we live out the "one another" commands of Scripture, "we get dressed as people who belong to other people."[9] The youth group jargon of not being a stumbling block to others has biblical grounds (Rom. 14:13). We have a responsibility to our brothers and sisters in Christ to behave in ways that build them up in their pursuit of godliness (Rom. 14:19–20). And—most importantly—we submit to a Father whose authority reaches even to our daily clothing choices. "To the child of God, the outfit choices on the rack are not without limits."[10]

Hill makes several good arguments for modesty that center on the idea that we tell a story with our dress and should make sure we're telling the truth. She acknowledges that modesty applies to both men and women, but also points out that the two genders are unique in their forms and should honor God in that uniqueness. "Covering certain parts doesn't deny the fact of our God-given sexuality or seek to diminish our beauty. To the contrary . . . treating these parts with modesty is a sign of honoring their importance."[11] As a man, I understand writing about this is taboo at best and asking to have stones thrown at me at worst, so I lean on Megan's words. She cites another wise woman, Elisabeth Elliot, quoting, "The fact that I am a woman does not make me a different kind of Christian, but the fact that I am a Christian makes me a different kind of woman."[12] So, Hill concludes, "God made you a woman. Dress accordingly."[13] Or, to include men as well, as my college pastor Dwayne Carson used to say, "For Christians, it should be different."

The goal of our lives should never be to express ourselves but rather to love God and our neighbor. None of us, regardless of gender, simply dress for ourselves. Whether we are consciously dressing for the approval of others, we don't live in isolation.

Our decisions (and in cases, our wardrobes) impact other people. Most of us remember the pressure of shopping for clothes in middle and high school, because what you wore was a social statement communicating your identity or affiliations. Depending on what you wore, you may have been received or rejected from certain groups. The reality is that even as adults, many of us still get dressed for these reasons, whether it means showing biceps, cleavage, or whatever body part one wants to be seen by others. There is often a performative element—a desire to communicate something about your identity. That message could be "Notice me, I'm single" or simply, "I'm in step with the latest trends." Personal style is a big part of our expressive culture, and I do not think it is inherently wrong, but for those of us following Christ, self-expression and admiration for our bodies isn't the goal. The love of God and neighbor is the goal, and it should impact every area of our lives, even when it doesn't make sense to the world and goes against our instincts to show something to everyone else. In his pastoral letters, the apostle John speaks to our struggle as believers as we seek not to drift towards the wisdom and values of this world out of misaligned affections. He wrote, "Do not love the world or the things in the world. If anyone loves the world, the love of the Father is not in him. For everything in the world—the lust of the flesh, the lust of the eyes, and the pride in one's possessions—is not from the Father, but is from the world" (1 John 2:15–16). John lists three categories of things "not from the Father":

The Lust of the Flesh

This can be rephrased as "I want to feel that." In our sinful state, we are prone to want to be desired, even to be *wanted* in a romantic way by others, even if we have no intention of that desire culminating in any actual physical activity. We've all seen friends who post bathing suit pictures on social media with comment sections littered with fire emojis and dramatic captions like "stunning" or "gorgeous." Human nature wants to feel everything that comes with a large thread of comments responding positively to a post showcasing one's physical appearance. In fact, for some people it is normal to post a staged picture in a particular swimsuit for that actual purpose—to feed the lust of the flesh. It's a dopamine hit, and it can be addictive. The desire to feel attractive is one of the biggest hindrances to the modesty conversation. My pushback is not to say that a person shouldn't care about his or her appearance but rather to question the underlying motivation behind what is worn, shared, or exposed.

The Lust of the Eyes

This can be rephrased as "I want to have that." Someone driven by outward perception or the need to always stay on top of trends might appear confident, but often this is nowhere near the case. Those who are truly sure of themselves as Christians are confident in Christ. Instead of needing to be the Pinterest-perfect hostess or have the admiration of throngs of Instagram followers, Christians should look to Christ and His church for guidance and belonging. But here is what is so complicated: this is viewed as a Sunday school answer. Many believers still wrestle internally with wanting to be seen and known, but the answer cannot be found in anything apart from Christ.

John reminded us that "the world with its lust is passing away" (1 John 2:17). Turning our eyes in hunger or loneliness to the things of this world will not ultimately satisfy. We have access to more information than ever before in human history, and yet we spend the nights scrolling, refreshing, browsing, and trying to find something worth loving or following—someone to show us how to look, how to act, how to feel complete. Something in us thinks that if we keep scrolling, we will find happiness. But there is a different way to use our eyes, and that is "keeping our eyes on Jesus" (Heb. 12:2). Jesus is worthy of our fixed gaze. He will never pass away or disappoint. And He will actually love us back.

Pride in One's Possessions

My friend once told me that she "worked really hard to get this body, so I'll show it off as I please." The first two lusts (of the flesh and of the eyes) feed into this final one. Since I want to feel that and have that, I will show what I need to show. My friend was staking her claim in response to some pushback she received from Christian girlfriends about the pictures she was posting online. This is also prevalent with men, some of whom exercise not for health but for applause. (Have you ever noticed that those guys always have their shirts off whenever given the opportunity?) Men and women alike who feel they have earned the right to show off their bodies must ask themselves why it's so important to them. Self-expression is the battle cry of a generation, and for a lost world this makes perfect sense. What else is there? Yet for the believer, expressions of self shouldn't be anchored to selfish use of bodies that aren't ours to begin with: "Don't you know that your body is a temple of the Holy Spirit who is in you, whom you have from God? You are not your own, for you were bought at a price. So glorify God with your body" (1 Cor. 6:19–20). Sam Allberry, commenting on this truth, wrote that "if our bodies belong to Jesus, then the only one who needs to be pleased with our bodies is Jesus. And he is far easier to please in this regard than our culture. . . . Paul urges us to 'Present your bodies as a living sacrifice, holy and acceptable to God' (Rom. 12:1). A body that is pleasing to Jesus is a body that is offered to him and given to his purposes."[14]

Now, to return to an important disclaimer, women are not to be blamed for men acting on lustful impulses. This extends well beyond consensual activity to rape and other forms of sexual abuse, which should never be attributed to what someone was wearing. This type of harmful—and frankly demonic—thinking should be outright rejected by anyone with a pulse, let alone a follower of Jesus Christ. Yet we should each still be considerate of how to conduct ourselves to not make it easier for others to sin. Megan Hill writes, "This also means we will do everything in our power to promote holiness in the hearts and minds of our fellow believers. We are 'called to be saints together' (1 Cor. 1:2). We don't want our clothing to be an occasion for jealousy or for lust. It may not be our responsibility if someone sins, but it is our privilege to help prevent it. Because we love the saints—because *Christ* loves the saints—we are willing to choose our clothing to encourage the holiness of the community."[15]

We are certainly a peculiar people as the body of Christ. Our logic will never make sense to the wisdom of this world, as God's glory and love of neighbor drive our lives more than self-expression or momentary fulfillment. We strive together to be a people who "decide never to put a stumbling block or pitfall in the way of your brother or sister" (Rom. 14:13). After all, we are not our own.

It's one thing to take to Twitter with our convictions, but it's another thing entirely to work it out in our own homes with those we are called to shepherd. As a dad of sons myself, I don't have to worry about a swimsuit issue coming in the mail once a year, but I do have to deal with the onslaught of images coming at my kids daily. TV, ads, websites, and even scrolling through social media feeds of their friends can lead them down a path far away from Job's commitment of not looking lustfully after a woman. Rather than trying to shield them from the world constantly, I want to teach them to live in this world faithfully. One way I am leading my boys to do this is by trying to create in my household a high level of respect toward women. My sons know that disrespecting their mother or speaking harshly to their sister is absolutely unacceptable. I hope that, as they grow, they will see their responsibility to be men of God who value women and see them not as objects of lust but as fellow image bearers worthy of respect and honor. I pray that my daughter, as she receives respect from her brothers and watches how I interact with my wife, will also form an expectation of how boys should treat her. I do not apologize for this and believe it is essential for my boys to understand that they will treat women differently than they treat men. We do not pretend men and women are the same. We are distinct from one another and that is for God's glory. Yes, I try to protect them from the sexualization of the world, but even more, I want to lead them to see the world differently, to understand that they have a responsibility not only for their own sister but also for their sisters in Christ.

LIE NO. 4:
"Gay is Okay"

I recently saw a social media "coming-out party" of sorts. A somewhat public Christian figure staged a photo of himself with an announcement that he was a gay man. Sprinkled into his announcement caption were words along the lines of "being who God made him to be," and I was surprised to see the support and applause of many Christian ministry leaders, authors, and public figures in the replies. These same people claim to believe that God created marriage to be between a man and a woman and that the Bible has authority—the same Bible that clearly calls homosexuality a sin. What is going on?

It used to be that Christians generally maintained that a homosexual lifestyle was in opposition to biblical sexual ethics. Now, you can find Christians who not only affirm LGBTQ lifestyles but celebrate them. Even those who hold to orthodox evangelical beliefs can become very squirmy and uncomfortable, unwilling to express what the Bible says regarding the matter. We have begun to believe the world's rhetoric that sexual desires define a person's identity and that individuals have sole authority to determine their own sexual identity based on the desires they experience.

What was once reserved for a progressive branch of Christianity, where other traditional doctrines (such as the virgin birth and salvation through Jesus Christ alone) were already frequently called into question, has now made its way into evangelicalism. "Gay is okay" is no longer reserved for progressive Christians who make gay affirmation a central tenet of their churches. We're now seeing this creep into churches that have historically held more conservative values. We can't have a discussion on sexual ethics in a post-purity culture evangelical context without addressing the dramatic shift taking place regarding churches and same-sex relationships. As culture continues to move toward a post-gender mindset, those who wish to expound a biblical worldview that points to the work of Christ will need to be clearer than ever regarding what the Scriptures say about homosexuality. Unfortunately, such churches are now the minority. I believe there are two primary types of churches that have departed from traditional biblical teaching on the matter: those who explicitly support it and those who implicitly support it by refusing to address it.

THE "LOVE IS LOVE" CHURCH

Churches in this category are now prominent in mainline denominations and simply assert that the Bible is outdated or wrong regarding homosexuality. This thinking has crept into the leadership of some evangelical churches under the guise of wanting to "love and affirm our neighbors." This camp believes that as long as a person truly loves, his or her sexual preference is irrelevant and affirmed by God. Love is all you need. In fact, some argue that speaking against any sort of lifestyle contradicts Jesus' example of compassion toward others. The primary issue, however, is not sexuality. The issue is whether the Bible has authority. If the Bible is wrong, ignorant, or irrelevant, why believe it at all? Why be a Christian if you have no confidence in the Scriptures and mock biblical authority? As Macklemore rapped in his 2012 song "Same Love" about those who have confidence in the authority of the Bible, "We paraphrase a book written thirty-five-hundred years ago."[1] If you're a professing believer and that's the view you have of the Holy Bible, you may be wasting your time.

Many years ago, I served as an intern to the senior minister at a church in suburban Washington DC. He was leading a mass exodus from the Episcopal Church to form the Anglican Communion in the United States. Their impetus for leaving was the 2003 ordination of Gene Robinson as bishop of the state of New Hampshire diocese. Robinson had previously left his wife to enter a same-sex relationship, and all during his tenure as a priest. The church's response? Let's make him a bishop!

Leaving a denomination is a massive decision, and in this case, the Episcopalian diocese owned the church building. This was not as simple as "They ordained Robinson, so we're leaving tomorrow." Lawyers were involved and preparation was required. The church held a town hall style meeting as soon as the news broke of Robinson becoming the new bishop, and I will never forget the opening words of the senior minister as he stepped to the podium to address this local church that was first organized in the late 1700s. I was sitting there as a young intern, expecting a sermon about same-sex relationships, when he said, "The decision to leave the Episcopal Church is not about homosexuality, it is about the Bible." It was a mic-drop moment and those in the room seemed to get the significance of his opening comments, as they erupted into a loud ovation. This wasn't some sort of conservative anti-gay rally or protest. This decision for the church mattered, because the Bible mattered. They weren't leaving the Episcopal Church because they hated gay people but because they believed the Bible was God's Word and felt that it had not only been compromised but directly disobeyed. This particular minister was willing to recognize the writing on the wall—his denomination had drawn a line in the sand by ordaining someone actively living in sin, and he didn't want his congregation to be on the wrong side of it.

THE "MC HAMMER" CHURCH

This second category of church, which I've dubbed the "MC Hammer" church, is growing, innovative, young, trendy, has an amazing band and an A-list "communicator," and stays upbeat by following the unspoken rule: "Can't touch this." What do they believe about homosexuality? They won't say; you can't touch that. These churches will occasionally do sermon series on marriage and family, but they pretty much steer clear of addressing sexual ethics in relation to homosexuality. Or, if they do address it, they will give apologies and disclaimers out of fear of upsetting the young majority. This might have worked a few years ago (even as recently as the publication of my last book, in which I told a story about a friend who attended an evangelical church and didn't know that the pastor didn't affirm her homosexual lifestyle), but now the pro-gay revolution isn't buying it. There's a type of reckoning, and people and organizations are being called to transparency on where they stand.

One website, www.churchclarity.org, lists churches' stances concerning homosexuality. The three categories are Clear, Unclear, and Undisclosed. The church I pastor is listed as "Clear: Non-Affirming in their LGBTQ policy." Another church in our community that is certainly evangelical and orthodox in theology is listed as "undisclosed" in their LGBTQ policy. While the website certainly has issue with non-affirming churches like mine, there is a preference for being clear. The headings on the website's "About" page assert that "Ambiguity is Harmful" and that "Clarity is Reasonable."[2] The strategy of silence is viewed as harmful by the very group that helps gay people find affirming churches. Yet most MC Hammer churches likely assume they are being loving in their silence.

I sincerely hope all churches welcome and embrace all people, because all people are loved by God and made in His image. But what has made this conversation virtually impossible is that many people equate affirmation of the human being with affirmation of his or her lifestyle. I think the Bible effectively separates the two. We are all loved by God and we are all called to repent of our sin, not label ourselves by it. And eventually, we'll all have to realize that there is no neutral zone on this issue for Christians. Even logistically, churches will have to sort out their stance when a practicing homosexual wants to be in leadership, be in an open relationship with someone of the same sex, or have the pastor perform a wedding ceremony.

I see more and more Christians approaching homosexuality based largely on emotions and their relationships with others. The sexual revolution has been paraded in front of them for their entire lives. Young generations don't know a world without gay marriage, pride month, and an all-out cultural celebration of all things gay. This is the generation that saw the White House lit up in rainbow colors after the Supreme Court Obergefell decision, which legalized same-sex marriage in America. They don't know a world without same-sex wedding photos popping up in their Instagram feed and gay romantic relationships being normalized on TV. It is more normal than in previous generations to have openly gay friends and family members. It is not uncommon to hear a Christian, especially a young adult or college student, reply to any question about their views concerning homosexuality with, "Well, I have gay friends," or, "My cousin is gay."

Relationships certainly matter, and I want to be sympathetic to the human nature that wants to avoid creating conflict with or disappointment from people we care about, but what is interesting to me in the homosexuality conversation is how it appears to be the one issue where you aren't allowed to "go there" with a family member or friend. Beyond even bringing it up as contrary to God's design, homosexuality is something you must fully affirm, otherwise you will be deemed unsupportive of your loved ones and charged with rejecting who they are at their core. I know Christians with gay children who had never affirmed homosexuality as an acceptable lifestyle for a Christian, but as a result of their son or daughter coming out as homosexual, they've now changed their social media profiles to a rainbow design during pride month. The relational pressure is real. The biggest fear parents often have when it comes to their adult children is that something could happen to damage the relationship. If that means compromising Christian convictions for the sake of peace, so be it. I don't think abandoning the faith is usually the intention, and perhaps some parents wrestle grievously over this tension, but we have been so influenced by an American version of Christianity that we no longer count the cost of following Jesus.

Jesus said, "The one who loves a father or mother more than me is not worthy of me; the one who loves a son or daughter more than me is not worthy of me. And whoever doesn't take up his cross and follow me is not worthy of me" (Matt. 10:37–38). Salvation is free, but following Jesus isn't cheap. In fact, it is so costly that we are expected to reorder our very lives and, if necessary, be cut off from our families. Jesus was asked, "What is the greatest commandment?" and He gave a direct answer: "Love the Lord your God with all your heart, with all your soul, and with all your mind. This is the greatest and most important command. The second is like it: Love your neighbor as yourself. All the Law and the Prophets depend on these two commands" (Matt. 22:37–40). In answering the question, Jesus gave out a figurative gold and silver medal by letting His hearers know there is an actual winner for our top allegiance. "Love the Lord your God." He stated clearly, "This is the greatest and most important command." Scripture explains what it means to keep the gold medal commandment by telling us exactly "what love for God is: to keep his commands" (1 John 5:3).

It is easy to think we are loving our neighbor and rightfully living out the second greatest commandment by affirming homosexuality (or any sexual behavior that diverges from biblical commands), especially given the fact that we are told that to be non-affirming is to deny personhood, inflict trauma, and reject an individual altogether. But here is the reality: If loving God means keeping His commandments, we are never keeping the second greatest commandment if it causes us to break the first. It isn't loving our neighbor if it results in going against what God has said in His Word. Encouraging people to persist in sin has real and eternal consequences, and it does not have to be a personal attack to call someone to repent and trust in the goodness and sufficiency of Jesus. This is in no way rejecting someone! It is loving them.

The way we best keep the silver medal commandment is by keeping the gold medal commandment. A common justification for avoiding biblical teaching on sexuality is that we should "just focus on Jesus." But it was Jesus who pointed to the creation and marriage of Adam and Eve when asked about marriage in Matthew 19, and it is Jesus whose death is given as the model for husbands to love their wives "as Christ loved the church" (Eph. 5:25). Focusing on Jesus certainly means more than talking about heterosexual marriage, but biblical marriage isn't detached from His person and teaching.

Why is all of this such a big deal? Because people's lives and eternities are at stake. Buckle up, we're going to Romans 1. In the introduction of the book of Romans, Paul explains the guilt of all people before a holy God and gives a specific example of what this rebellion looks like.

> Claiming to be wise, they became fools and exchanged the glory of the immortal God for images resembling mortal man, birds, four-footed animals, and reptiles.
> Therefore God delivered them over in the desires of their hearts to sexual impurity, so that their bodies were degraded among themselves. They exchanged the truth of God for a lie, and worshiped and served what has been created instead of the Creator, who is praised forever. Amen.
> For this reason God delivered them over to disgraceful passions. Their women exchanged natural sexual relations for unnatural ones. The men in the same way also left natural relations with women and were inflamed in their lust for one another. Men committed shameless acts with men and received in their own persons the appropriate penalty of their error.
> And because they did not think it worthwhile to acknowledge God, God delivered them over to a corrupt mind so that they do what is not right. They are filled with all unrighteousness, evil, greed, and wickedness. They are full of envy, murder, quarrels, deceit, and malice. They are gossips, slanderers, God-haters, arrogant, proud, boastful, inventors of evil, disobedient to parents, senseless, untrustworthy, unloving, and unmerciful. Although they know God's just sentence—that those who practice such things deserve to die—they not only do them, but even applaud others who practice them. (Rom. 1:22–32)

Paul is painting for the Romans a picture of the state of their surrounding world. One where God has been rejected and lawless human affections have taken over, where people worship what was created rather than their Creator. The passage begins and ends with past tense descriptions like "They exchanged the truth of God for a lie" and "God delivered them over" framing present tense descriptions like "they do not do what is right" and "They are filled with all unrighteousness." "They" is pretty broad while examples of homosexuality are pretty specific, but I believe we are intended to interpret "they" to refer to godless people in the surrounding culture, not all of whom would be engaged in homosexual activity. So what does this mean? While Paul is not saying that homosexuality stands alone as the worst of sins, the passage clearly presents homosexuality as an example of what it looks like to rebel against the Creator. It is the outworking of exchanging the worship of God for the worship of something else. It is directly contrary to the one flesh union of a husband and a wife that is intended to point us to the union of Jesus and His bride, the church.

This is why I am so urgent on the matter as a pastor, Christian, and friend. Homosexuality is complete rebellion against God—in other words, whether they are wanted or not, acting on those feelings is not blessed or permissible in God's eyes. There is never one instance in Scripture where same-sex relationships are affirmed, applauded, or treated as normal. (This kind of sexual perversion resulted in the literal destruction of Sodom and Gomorrah.) Paul makes it clear to the Corinthian believers that "the unrighteous will not inherit God's kingdom." He tells them, "Do not be deceived," as "no sexually immoral people, idolaters, adulterers, or males who have sex with males, no thieves, greedy people, drunkards, verbally abusive people, or swindlers will inherit God's kingdom" (1 Cor. 6:9–10). Yes, that list includes examples of immorality besides homosexuality, but homosexuality is certainly listed.

People often ask why God would create someone with desires that He would also consider sinful. Why would He make someone a certain way and then condemn the person for being that way?

The answer is that God doesn't actually do that. We all have sinful desires, and none of them are God's fault. Neither does He want us to label ourselves by them. We must go back to Romans 1, which shows us what happened as a result of Adam and Eve's disobedience in Genesis 3. The fall of man has affected every area of our lives, especially our desires. The book of James even tells us that God doesn't tempt us to sin; on the contrary, we are tempted by our own inmost desires which, when "fully grown," lead to death (James 1:14). Our desires and passions are flawed from the very moment we are able to form them, and God is not ignorant of this. He sees our truest selves, which is why the Psalmist writes, "May the words of my mouth and the meditation of my heart be acceptable to you, LORD, my rock and my Redeemer" (Ps. 19:14). We need God's help to have desires that are pure.

> We are all called to the same sexual purity and we are all called to put to death our sinful desires.

In addition, we must distinguish between the Christian experiencing same-sex attraction yet walking in holiness and the person identifying as a Christian yet living a homosexual lifestyle. We can agree with Scripture against our fleshly desires. And—to live as Christians—we must. In Romans 1, Paul includes homosexuality as one of "the desires of their hearts" in the context of sexual sin (v. 24). He also references "disgraceful passions" (v. 26). Same-sex relationships are described as unnatural (v. 27), not as desires that should be legitimized based on the fact that they exist. Thus, it is important in this context to know that the goal for the Christian with same-sex desires is not heterosexuality, but holiness. The pursuit of holiness will not exist independently of daily repentance of one's desires. But the good news of the gospel is that following Christ is equally inclusive and equally exclusive to all people, regardless of their individual weaknesses or tendencies. We are all called to the same sexual purity and we are all called to put to death our sinful desires. This applies to the heterosexual single person, to the married person, and to the person experiencing same-sex attraction. Regardless of how the Church may have fumbled in this regard, the *Bible* does not discriminate against any particular kind of sinner—we all must come and fall at the feet of Christ. For the Christian, sinful desires are not inherent to one's identity; rather they present a daily battle as we seek to "walk by the Spirit, and you will certainly not carry out the desire of the flesh" (Gal. 5:16).

For this reason, I think we must reject the title of "gay Christian." When you're in Christ, no other thing forms your identity. I cannot find any justification in the Scriptures for any sinful lifestyle to be used as a modifier or qualification of what kind of believer you are—we don't (or at least should never) have "adulterous Christians" or "murderous Christians," as though those two things can actively coexist. Yet there are people who desire to normalize the tension between Christian beliefs and gay lifestyles by creating an environment in which one can be both.

In recent years, The Revoice Conference and organization have emerged, describing their mission as "supporting, encouraging, and empowering gay, lesbian, same-sex-attracted, and other LGBT Christians so they can flourish while observing the historic, Christian doctrine of marriage and sexuality."[3] Gene Burrus acknowledges that "to many on the evangelical scene, I'm sure it seems as if Revoice represents a progressive shift. However, in the context of its . . . origins [diverging from a more progressive wave that affirms LGBTQ lifestyles], Revoice was a shift *toward* a conservative sexual ethic."[4] As an answer to loneliness in this population, some Christians advocate for what has been called "spiritual friendships," in which people can "[renounce] their erotic desires" by forming "close and even vowed or covenanted friendships with other Christians of the same sex."[5] In short, this is very troubling to me. We wouldn't tell a heterosexual Christian woman to live with and enter a serious covenantal friendship with a man she sexually desires but can't have sex with or marry. It's just not healthy and doesn't make any sense if the goal is purity and obedience to Christ. Instead, as I have and will advocate elsewhere in this book, the local church is the blessed and original forum for Christians of all kinds to find true community, regardless of marital status.

A church member who is a single adult and a Bible study leader once came to me to let me know he struggled with same-sex attraction. He wanted to be honest with me and wondered if his same-sex attraction disqualified him as a group leader. Fully aware of the risk he took in showing such vulnerability, I affirmed his commitment to Christ, as he assured me that he was not acting on these attractions, that he held to orthodox Christian teaching regarding marriage, and that he believed homosexuality to be sinful. I told him that, based on his convictions and lifestyle choices, he was certainly able to continue serving his church as a leader. This is what I would have said to any single young man experiencing sexual temptation of the heterosexual variety as well. Are you walking in sin or have you changed your beliefs on biblical sexual ethics? I told him there was one "catch." In following Jesus, he should reject a gay lifestyle altogether, which means not dating someone of the same sex, even if it was celibate. He affirmed that request as something he believed himself and added that he rejected the notion of identifying as a "gay Christian."

My primary point is that the Bible is clear that homosexuality is a sin, but that does not mean that those with same-sex desires are disqualified from partaking in God's kingdom, so long as they— like every other Christian—submit their desires to the lordship of Christ. In regard to sex, every Christian has the same two options:

celibacy or monogamous, heterosexual, covenantal marriage. We must hold fast to the truth of Galatians 5: "For the flesh desires what is against the Spirit, and the Spirit desires what is against the flesh; these are opposed to each other" (v. 17). No Christian can identify with desires that are out of step with what God has declared to be sinful. They are opposed to one another. Paul lists some of those desires that are opposed to God, including sexual immorality, moral impurity, and promiscuity (Gal. 5:19). He calls them the "works of the flesh." Those who are in Christ don't continue to identify by those desires because "those who belong to Christ Jesus have crucified the flesh with its passions and desires" (Gal. 5:24). I want to be sympathetic toward the journey of my brothers and sisters with same-sex temptations, and I am not in denial of the difficulty of that journey. But in a sense, we're all in this together. All believers must pick up their crosses to follow Jesus. Rather than living as a "gay Christian," someone experiencing same-sex attraction should work out his or her salvation by crucifying the flesh out of a daily, growing affection for Christ.

Jackie Hill Perry tells her experience of coming to repentance from a lesbian relationship, writing, "I loved my girlfriend too much not to be appalled at the prospect of laying aside not only the way I loved but also who I loved . . . I loved her, and she loved me—but God loved me more. So much so that he wouldn't have me going about the rest of my life convinced that a creature's love was better than a King's."[6] Jackie acknowledges that God wasn't calling her to be "straight," but holy: "Homosexuality might have been my loudest sin, but it was not my *only* sin. God was not about setting me free from one form of slavery only to leave me enslaved to other idols. By calling me to himself, he was after my whole heart . . . so my repentance would not be singular. That night, I knew that it wasn't just my lesbianism that had me at odds with God—it was my entire heart."[7] In breaking up with her girlfriend,

Jackie recalled, "'I just . . . gotta live for God now,' I said with a tear-broken voice. A new identity was to come after I hung up. I had no idea what would come next or how I'd have the power to resist everything I'd once lived for, but I knew that if Jesus was God and if God was mighty to save, then surely, God would be mighty to keep. And 10 years later, he is still keeping this girl godly."[8]

This kind of story makes zero sense to the world and is seen as quintessential oppressive religion: that someone like Jackie would have to endure the pain of a breakup with someone she loved and had been in a serious relationship with. Jackie picked up her cross that day, and it was based on her belief in the truth that Jesus was God and had saved her soul. The church must realize that the world will always see us as borderline insane or bigoted or homophobic when it comes to believing what the Scriptures say about homosexuality. To the world, it is absurd to suggest that two men in a committed loving relationship are in the wrong. "Love is love," after all. The difference for Christians is that we don't define love apart from who God is and what He has commanded His people to do. It matters greatly who you love, because God created the context where that love is to be practiced and displayed, and that is in the union of a lifelong covenant between a husband and a wife.

It is important to note that our message is not, "Everyone be a heterosexual!" Our message, like what Jackie believes, is that Jesus saves, transforms, and sustains. One who is transformed by Jesus will submit their desires to His commands, believing that His plan and commands are sufficient. We can keep these things in mind:

- We do not have to go around God for purpose and identity. Those things are found in Jesus, who makes all things new.
- We are never promised a life without temptation.

- We are promised, in Christ, a high priest who will sympathize with our weaknesses, because Jesus has been tempted but did not sin.
- The great truth for all believers is that through Christ we can "approach the throne of grace with boldness, so that we may receive mercy and find grace to help us in time of need" (Heb. 4:15–16).

There is a different way than being a Love is Love church or an MC Hammer church, and that is being a gospel-centered church. These churches aren't afraid to call sin, sin, because they know Jesus came to die for sinners. As Paul wrote regarding sexual sin and immorality, "And some of you used to be like this. But you were washed, you were sanctified, you were justified in the name of the Lord Jesus Christ and by the Spirit of our God" (1 Cor. 6:11). What incredible words! You used to be like this, but Jesus washed you. In fact, you aren't guilty of your sin anymore because you were justified, declared innocent. Jesus, who was without sin, was condemned to death in our place. It is this gospel, being bought with a price, that fuels Paul's charge: "Flee sexual immorality! Every other sin a person commits is outside the body, but the person who is sexually immoral sins against his own body. Don't you know that your body is a temple of the Holy Spirit who is in you, whom you have from God? You are not your own, for you were bought at a price. So glorify God with your body" (1 Cor. 6:18–20).

Gospel-centered churches aren't afraid to enter the ring of fire regarding the hot topics and taboo issues of the day. Like Paul stepping into the Areopagus in the heart of Athens, we have a message to our culture, and it is that Jesus is Lord. He is good and He knows best. In his letter, Jude reminds the reader of the fate of Sodom and Gomorrah and the "surrounding towns," who committed sexual immorality and serve as an example by undergoing the punishment of eternal fire (1:7). This verse and historic reminder should stop the Christian in his or her tracks regarding the fate of those who practice sexual sin. According to Genesis, for these cities it was explicit homosexual sin (19:4–5). How can Christians read such verses and conclude that we shouldn't address this sin and simply "love"? I can't think of something more loving than to plea for someone to be reconciled to God through Christ by repenting of his or her sins in faith. You may know a gay couple who are nice people and seem to have a better relationship than many heterosexual couples you know. But let us not become the people described at the end of Romans 1: "Although they know God's just sentence—that those who practice such things deserve to die—they not only do them, but even applaud others who practice them" (v. 32).

What an indictment. Instead, may the church live by these words from Jude's letter: "Keep yourselves in the love of God, waiting expectantly for the mercy of our Lord Jesus Christ for eternal life. Have mercy on those who waver; save others by snatching them from the fire; have mercy on others but with fear, hating even the garment defiled by the flesh" (1:21–23).

8

LIE NO. 5:
"My Bedroom
is My Business"

A friend of mine invited me to catch up over lunch. As we looked at the menu, I could tell he was excited to tell me something. "So, I've been hanging out with someone," he said. He went on to tell me that the girl he had been out with a couple times was really great, that they shared similar values, and that he thought there was potential for a long-term relationship. "The sex has been really good too," he added, as the waiter awkwardly told us he would give us a few more minutes to look at the menu. While I appreciate that my friend can be so matter-of-fact with me knowing my convictions and that I'm a pastor, I gave him a blank stare across the table, hoping he could translate it as "C'mon man, you're killing me." Sensing my reaction, he quickly said, "I mean, you want to make sure you're compatible going forward, right? Imagine having to find out you aren't sexually compatible when you're already engaged or married!"

My first thought was wondering what people think "sexually compatible" even means, knowing that my friend was not making this concept up but was feeding off of a very common notion. Today, society's unwritten pre-marriage checklist includes checking for sexual compatibility. But even aside from the obvious fact that it requires pre-marital sex, sexual compatibility is not something Christians need to worry about. Sex in marriage is something learned together, an experience for the inexperienced, as they strive to keep the instruction of Hebrews 13:4: "Marriage is to be honored by all and the marriage bed kept undefiled."

As has been a theme in the aftermath of purity culture, well-intentioned oddities in Christian culture have led to overcorrections. I see two competing pendulum swings: first, from prudence to an all-out exposition of married sex, and second, a trauma-based recoiling from biblical commands on sexual requirements between spouses.

In past generations, it was taboo to speak about the marriage bedroom, which lived under the banner of "TMI." But in more recent years, even in Christian spheres, a counter swing turned sex in marriage into its own cottage industry. I remember sitting in the conference that took Christian culture by storm in the early 2000s, the Song of Solomon Conference. This was a crash course, two-day conference that explicitly taught the context of the book of Song of Solomon (also called Song of Songs in some translations). I remember it being so awkward sitting next to guy and girl friends alike during those sessions, all of us unmarried college students, hearing a sixty-year-old man talk about having sex with his wife. I don't recall any mention of Christ and the church or any theology from the Song of Songs, just lots of talk about sex. To be fair, the intimacy shared between a husband and a wife is present throughout the Old Testament poetry book, where sex and romance in the context of marriage are viewed as good, holy, and proper. But we

had swung from only hearing about sex as something not to do unless you're married to sex being expounded from every page of Song
of Songs in an auditorium packed with single college students.

This candid approach to teaching on Christian marriage took
off. Sermons on sex became the norm, especially in contemporary,
seeker-style churches. I remember a billboard on a main road in
the city where I live advertising an upcoming sermon series. The
billboard depicted a bedroom with a woman's leg hanging outside
of the sheet, the title "Best Sex Ever," and the dates of the series
painted across the sign. One Texas pastor challenged the married
couples in his congregation to "Seven Days of Sex." The "SEXPER-
IMENT," which later became the title of his book, was designed
to "[show] people that sex in marriage is more than just sex, and
it's more than a chore."[1] In his words, "While society has taken sex
too far, the church hasn't taken it far enough."[2] In an interview, the
pastor added, "We want married people to see their bedroom for
what it is—a magnet of stability, something that draws them away
from the dangerous pull of lust that derails so many couples."[3]
While that statement at face value isn't off base, the methodol-
ogy was a bit odd. In 2012, he livestreamed a twenty-four-hour
cuddling session with his wife in a bed on the roof of his church
building.[4] Sermons on sex became marketing ploys to get people
to church. The swing was so intense it would have made Mickey
Mantle's Louisville Slugger jealous.

Into the midst of this movement came Mark Driscoll, a church
planter-turned-megachurch pastor in Seattle who rose to popularity in the early 2000s. Driscoll, known for bluntness and
brashness, took that same trademark approach toward the topics
of marriage and sex. In the book he coauthored with his wife, *Real
Marriage: The Truth about Sex, Friendship, and Life Together*, a significant amount of space is used to address sex and the question of
"Can We _____?"[5] This section aimed to answer questions

about the permissibility of various sexual acts for Christian married couples. Certain acts were addressed that I never would have considered going into detail about in print or in a sermon, but the book attracted serious attention. Christians apparently wanted to hear about sex, and there was now big industry in talking about it in specific detail. Even for Christians, apparently, sex sells.

In the summer of 2021, *Christianity Today* began releasing a podcast called *The Rise and Fall of Mars Hill,* which focused on the story of the collapse of the church Driscoll pastored as well as his own downfall. One episode that received significant attention and sparked much conversation upon its release was episode 5, "The Things We Do To Women." In his recap of the episode, one blogger claimed the podcast "documents Driscoll manipulating Scripture to paint a reductionistic picture of sex that is pornographic and a far cry from the sacred gospel-adorning marital intimacy presented in Scripture."[6] *Christianity Today* described Driscoll as "elevating women as Christian pornographic ideals."[7] Driscoll was known for crass and dismissive comments about women and their appearances or sexual obligations. At a training for church planters, he told an audience of pastors' wives that they held the "most important job" in a new church. That job, according to Driscoll, was "having sex with the church planter."[8] In 2006, after evangelist Ted Haggard was caught with male prostitutes, Driscoll took to the internet to comment that "it is not uncommon to meet pastors' wives who really let themselves go. A wife who lets herself go and is not sexually available to her husband . . . is not responsible for her husband's sin, but she may not be helping him either."[9]

While Driscoll and Mars Hill had become an afterthought to many, the successful CT podcast reminded massive online audiences of influential preaching that objectified the role of a wife in marriage. Beth Moore, in a Tweet following the release of episode

5, claimed "this placing on the wife the responsibility of her husband's faithfulness by being his own personal p-rn star (& in the name of Jesus) was by no means championed by Mars Hill alone. It was prevalent."[10] What a tragedy for any woman to ever feel like the equivalent of an on-demand porn star in her marriage. Not to mention the complete impropriety of a pastor publicly shaming women for not having a physical appearance that he prefers. There is certainly a problem when a married woman is taught from the pulpit that she should meet every sexual whim and fantasy of her husband—or that the husband should be able to do whatever he wants, whenever he desires, and the wife must act or be a bad wife, setting him up for adultery.

An abusive teaching on sex may seem like a far cry from my single friend making sure he had enough "sexual chemistry" with the girl he was dating. But a consumeristic view of sex can creep into Christian marriages when people are sitting under this type of teaching. Does the Bible have things to say about spouses' sexual obligations to each other? Yes. But are they pornographic and domineering? Not at all.

Christianity Today's exposé on Driscoll's teaching has rekindled outrage across Christian social media, and deservedly so, but—as comes with evangelical culture—the over-corrective swing has taken place yet again. While the hypersexual objectivity that is still certainly taught must be denounced and rejected, I wonder if there is still a place for 1 Corinthians 7 to be taught in our churches. After all, the Bible speaks to sex, addressing it through a model that is neither secretive nor exhibitionist. In the New Testament especially, we see clear commands for a mutually-sacrificial and generous sexual relationship given without going into graphic detail about what that looks like from couple to couple.

So, what does the Bible say?

A HUSBAND AND WIFE HAVE SEXUAL OBLIGATIONS TO ONE ANOTHER.

Paul writes that "a husband should fulfill his marital duty to his wife, and likewise a wife to her husband" (1 Cor. 7:3). This duty and responsibility that husbands and wives have toward each other is not bad or oppressive but part of God's design, where we see that sex was not only created for procreation but also for pleasure. Paul continues, "A wife does not have the right over her own body, but her husband does. In the same way, a husband does not have the right over his own body, but his wife does" (v. 4). This should not be shocking to those who believe that a husband and wife become one flesh, and it is important to note that this bodily belonging to each other in the marriage union is mutual.

MARITAL OBLIGATIONS SHOULD BE ANCHORED IN CHRIST'S EXAMPLE.

Husbands have clear commands from God concerning their ultimate responsibility to their wives, and that is that each husband must love his wife as Christ loved the church, giving himself up for her (Eph. 5:25). Elsewhere, in Philippians 2, we get further insight into what Jesus is like. Paul urges believers to "adopt the same attitude as that of Christ Jesus, who, existing in the form of God, did not consider equality with God as something to be exploited. Instead he emptied himself by assuming the form of a servant, taking on the likeness of humanity. And when he had come as a man, he humbled himself by becoming obedient to the point of death—even to death on a cross" (Phil. 2:5–8).

One can conclude that a husband loving his wife as Christ loved the church should—at the very least—be unselfish and gentle and never use any type of leadership position for his own personal gain or pleasure. In the context of sex, the wife should never feel as if she is an object or personal porn star. This is serious, as biblical commands have been twisted and used to justify sexual abuse within marriage. It is unthinkable to comprehend how one called to love his wife as Christ loved the church could ever force (or even attempt to force) his wife to engage in something she doesn't want to do or has refused, but sadly this does take place. Paul's words about the husband and wife each having rights over each other's bodies should be heard and interpreted in the context of the rest of Scripture's portrait of love and marriage, which is characterized by mutual care and oneness.

MARRIED OR UNMARRIED, THE CHRISTIAN'S BODY BELONGS TO GOD.

First and foremost, the Christian's understanding of the body should begin with the conviction that "you are not your own, for you were bought at a price. So glorify God with your body" (1 Cor. 6:19–20). The husband and wife's responsibility over the other's body remains under the belief that ultimately their bodies don't belong to them but to God. Sex in marriage should first be to the glory of God, who created marriage, gave couples the gift of sex, and redeemed our bodies through the death and resurrection of Jesus Christ. When we remember that our bodies first belong to God, sex is never just about the triumph of our personal needs and desires, especially over our own spouse. However, that also means that we as individual Christians have a responsibility to examine our own hearts when we want to ask for something or refuse something our spouse has suggested in the sexual relationship.

SOMETIMES OBEDIENCE MEANS DOING THINGS YOU DON'T WANT TO DO.

In our hypersensitive evangelical culture, I worry that pastors are no longer even allowed to anchor teaching in Paul's instruction in 1 Corinthians 7 (that we have a Christian duty regarding sex in marriage) without being regarded as misogynistic or abusive toward women. (As an aside, Paul was not married at the time of his writing to the Corinthian church, so he wasn't saying this from a selfish perspective.) But Paul states that "a husband should fulfill his marital duty to his wife, and likewise a wife to her husband" (1 Cor. 7:3). Sex in marriage is designed to be a delight, but it is also a duty. There is a role to fulfill and action to take, and it flows from a mutual desire for the other's good. Part of living an unselfish life in marriage is doing things you sometimes don't want to do. To suggest that spouses should be willing to give themselves sexually to each other even at times when they might not feel like it is nowhere near the same category as being forced against one's will to do something cruel or inappropriate. It also needs to be stated that it's not godly for a person to persist in his or her own desires against his or her spouse's will. This balance of biological impulses and appetites with biblical commands requires maturity, fellowship with each other, and Spirit-driven kindness. A godly marriage exhibits a mutual pursuit of unselfishness for the good of the other.

Paul commands married couples to "not deprive one another—except when you agree for a time, to devote yourselves to prayer" (1 Cor. 7:5). I have joked when preaching on this verse that whatever kind of prayer Paul is alluding to must have been the fastest prayer in the history of praying! The fact is that part of being a faithful spouse is engaging willingly in regular sexual activity. Are there factors that some couples must work through and overcome both emotionally and physically? Certainly, but there does not need to be a disclaimer given to appease every objection from a social media chorus that is held psychologically hostage to the world's understanding of self-autonomy and individualism. In other words, if you object to married couples being taught that they're supposed to have sex with each other, your opposition is with the Bible, not a particular preacher.

As I often say, marriage is significantly more than sex, but it is definitely not less. God created men and women biologically complementary to one another (in a literal, physical sense and in other ways), instituted marriage, and defined what it means to be one flesh. This same God has instructed husbands and wives not to deprive each other, as the man is to "love his wife as himself, and the wife is to respect her husband" (Eph. 5:33). Rosie Moore has a word for married couples regarding sex: "Sex may require effort, forethought and a fierce spiritual battle, but Christian marriages must reclaim this delightful gift from God for our own good and for his glory. To reject, neglect, or grumble against God's gift, is to reject the Lord himself."[11] In a Christian marriage, each of the two individuals, who are now one flesh, should commit to unselfishly meet their spouse's sexual needs. An important exception would be anything that goes against God's design and the covenant of marriage (such as a polygamous encounter) or anything that sincerely violates one's conscience. (There's a difference between something that might simply require courage for one spouse and something that he or she earnestly believes is not God-honoring.)

SEX IS SUPPOSED TO BE ENJOYABLE.

As we saw earlier, perhaps the most explicit positive sexual content in the Bible is found in Song of Songs, which has historically had mixed understandings as either completely allegorical to spiritual realities or primarily a celebration of physical human love. Recent interpretations argue that it's both. In an essay in digital theology journal *Themelios* on the Song of Songs, a writer asserts,

> So the Song asks the Christian husband and wife, "How's your love life? Is your wedding bed dead or alive? Is it as cold as a frozen pond in February or as hot as the Florida sand in August?" . . . This Song is God's provision to sustain loving marriages and renew loveless ones. It is his provision for increased intimacy that reflects the intimacy of Christ's love for the church, an intimacy that makes the world turn its head to view our marriages and say, "So, that's the gospel. What must I do to be made *wise* unto salvation?"[12]

One might ask if this commentary reads too much into the Song of Songs. Kyle Dillon states that if "the New Testament authors understood and applied the themes of the Song in a Christological direction, then it's right for us to do so as well."[13] But Dillon does argue that the Song can be properly interpreted as both allegorical and literal, because marriage itself is allegorical and literal.

Marriage is a metaphor for God's relationship to the people He has redeemed. Dillon remarks that this theme runs throughout the Scriptures: "Israel is . . . described as God's 'beloved' (Jer. 11:15; 12:7), with whom he enters into a marriage covenant (Ezek. 16:8)."[14] He adds that "when a Christian husband faithfully fulfills his role to lead and love his wife, and when a Christian wife fulfills her role to honor and respect her husband, it puts the gospel on display in a way that no other human institution can. Therefore, we're justified in saying that the Song of Songs is an allegory of Christ and the church, because marriage itself is designed as an allegory of Christ and the church."[15] This comes directly from Ephesians 5.

Sex in marriage is more than pleasure and fulfillment. It is about the glory of God. The goal of sex is not some worldly ideal of sexual compatibility that one must search for until found, but rather the glory of God in acting out what He has designed. Sex involves care for one's spouse and a servant-hearted approach of mutual unselfishness for the other's benefit. Churches must talk about sex in marriage, and not as a marketing ploy to shock and entertain the masses with a forbidden topic. Rather, by teaching the Scriptures in light of the broader story of the Bible, churches can guide us to see how God designed sex for His glory and our good. His authority reaches into the most private corners of our lives, and even our obedience there brings Him honor.

9

LIE NO. 6:
"Nobody Has to Know"

Though the lips of the forbidden woman drip honey
and her words are smoother than oil,
in the end she's as bitter as wormwood
and as sharp as a double-edged sword.

PROVERBS 5:3-4

This is the Bible's warning to the man tempted to commit adultery.

There is no nuance or negotiation, no disclaimer or exception, but rather a stern warning. This warning leads to a command, "Keep your way far from her. Don't go near the door of her house" (Prov. 5:8). When it comes to the sin of adultery, God doesn't play around. Perhaps no other sin displays a heart of idolatry more clearly than that of committing adultery. It is literally a breaking of a covenant and an assault on God's design for sex. Adultery in the literal sense is decisively dealt within the Old and New Testaments as sinful and prohibited by God. Adultery as a metaphor takes on a larger role in the storyline of the Bible, depicting the seriousness of the unfaithfulness of God's people to Him. Similarly to how the union of a husband and a wife displays the union of Christ and the church, adultery is the metaphor the Scriptures use to illustrate the betrayal committed when God's people love other gods by choosing to disobey Him.

To illustrate to the prophet Hosea what was taking place among God's people Israel, the Lord said to him, "Go and marry a woman of promiscuity, and have children of promiscuity, for the land is committing blatant acts of promiscuity by abandoning the LORD" (Hos. 1:2). God actually called this man to marry a promiscuous woman so he could feel the true pain of being cheated on by someone who was supposed to be committed to him. God's people were to see themselves as having affairs with other gods.

James directly rebuked his Jewish-Christian audience with the same metaphor, saying, "You adulterous people! Don't you know that friendship with the world is hostility toward God? So whoever wants to be the friend of the world becomes the enemy of God" (4:4). In a devotional commentary on this verse from James, Ligonier Ministries explains:

> The apostle labels his original audience as an adulterous people, despite there being no indication in the epistle that sexual sin was a significant problem for his Jewish-Christian addressees. This indicates that spiritual adultery is what James has in view. At the same time, however, there is no hint that James' original readers were guilty of some kind of crass, pagan idolatry. No, the lover the audience pursued was something more subtle than outright idolatry and was therefore more dangerous.[1]

That danger, James says, is friendship with the world. This is not the same as being a "friend of sinners" as Jesus was called, based on His compassion for the lost. The friendship James is referring to is a "designation for that system whose values, loves, and deeds are wholly at odds with what pleases our Creator."[2]

John explains this in his first epistle: "Do not love the world or the things in the world. If anyone loves the world, the love of the Father is not in him. For everything in the world—the lust of the flesh, the lust of the eyes, and the pride in one's possessions—is not from the Father, but is from the world" (1 John 2:15–16). As we looked at in an earlier chapter:

- **The lust of the flesh** is the desire to feel something. This can include wanting to feel attractive, wanted, or happy, and the temptation is to believe one must go around God and His Word in order to meet these desires.
- **The lust of the eyes** is when one wants to have something. Often it is simply wanting to have what someone else has, such as status, attention, and admiration. The person experiencing this lust finds him or herself tempted to believe that there is more to be gained by disobeying God than by obeying Him.
- **Pride in one's possessions** wants to show something. This can be misunderstood as wanting to show off one's material belongings, but that minimizes what truly motivates friendship with the world concerning one's possessions. What this pride wants to show is an appearance. The appearance of still being young, fun, accomplished, and desirable.

The love of the world is based on the false belief that the world has what we're looking for and can provide for our greatest emotional needs. This belief in the saving power of this world is summed up in the Bible as spiritual adultery. The spiritually adulterous are those who have rejected God and instead have followed after alluring and tempting things that are not God. The visible act of adultery committed by a husband or a wife shows us the invisible reality of God's people's rebellion against their Creator. It is the failure to uphold one's part in a covenant relationship.

Idolatry is so foolish that the Lord's response to it is sometimes sarcastic, allowing His people to see just how senseless they are being in their worship of gods that aren't real. Like here:

Their idols are silver and gold,
made by human hands.
They have mouths but cannot speak,
eyes, but cannot see.
They have ears but cannot hear,
noses, but cannot smell.
They have hands but cannot feel,
feet, but cannot walk.
They cannot make a sound with their throats.
(Ps. 115:4–7)

Or here:

All who make idols are nothing,
and what they treasure benefits no one.
Their witnesses do not see or know anything,
so they will be put to shame.
Who makes a god or casts a metal image
that benefits no one? (Isa. 44:9–10)

How foolish is idolatry! The Lord wants to make sure we know how ridiculous we are being when it comes to spiritual adultery.

With these examples in mind, we should consider the relationship between spiritual adultery and the outworking of idolatry in the form of literal, physical adultery. I've never met a married person who woke up one morning and announced, "I'm going to commit adultery today." In the same way, when the Hebrew people were led out from slavery in Egypt, and when they saw God bring down the plagues and conquer Pharaoh's army by the

> Physical adultery is the working out of spiritual adultery, believing the world is our friend before Christ.

miraculous parting of the Red Sea, I'm sure they weren't thinking, "Hey, as soon as we get a chance, let's build a calf out of gold and worship it." Rather, their sin came when they quickly grew impatient with God and with Moses's intercession for them. They felt their greatest needs were not being met in a timely manner. Samuel James claims that "adultery is alluring not because it makes good logical sense, but because we see in our imagination its offer of happiness, secrecy, thrill, and fulfillment."[3]

Physical adultery is the working out of spiritual adultery, believing the world is our friend before Christ. God has something much better for His people in how they use the gift of sex as He has designed it. Rather than being drawn to the lips of the forbidden woman mentioned in the early portion of Proverbs 5, God calls us to "drink water from your own cistern, water flowing from your own well" (v. 15). He then shows us the beauty of the gift of sex and the great pleasure He has created for His people as they participate in it as He intended:

They should be for you alone
and not for you to share with strangers.
Let your fountain be blessed,
and take pleasure in the wife of your youth.

A loving deer, a graceful doe—
let her breasts always satisfy you;
be lost in her love forever. (Prov. 5:17–19)

In His grand design, God has something far better for husbands and wives than doing something permanent in a temporary encounter or relationship. Instead, He has given them "the wife of one's youth." Of course, this absolutely applies in reverse, as an instruction for wives to remain faithful to their husbands as well. But this should quell any misleading belief that we can "marry the wrong person" or that breaking marriage vows to pursue someone besides my spouse is okay because "God wants me to be happy." It's simply not biblical.

I have always seen adultery as the most childish behavior. As a dad of three kids, I know full well that one of the telltale signs of sinful behavior is the need to be sneaky. When my middle child was three years old, my wife was cleaning through his closet one day and found a half-consumed two-liter bottle of soda. Somehow, he had snatched it from our counter unseen, hidden it in his closet, and had been sneaking swigs of the forbidden sugar drink when no one was looking. We laughed because he was only three and had pulled off this undercover mission on his own, but we also saw his sinful nature on display. Jump to adulthood and we have married people with professional careers and major responsibilities living their lives like children, sneaking around taking swigs from a forbidden fountain. The entire process is done in secrecy because the people involved know it is shameful. Some people go to absurd lengths to hide and maintain affairs.

There has been much written about certain things that trigger affairs and much advice given about guardrails that supposedly help "affair-proof"[4] a marriage. While I think such advice can be helpful and can cause a couple to become aware of certain issues in their marriage that could make one vulnerable to temptation, I think that approach ultimately misses the point. Marriage is not primarily designed to meet your needs. If marriage was designed to meet your needs, what happens when those felt needs aren't met? The wisdom of this world would suggest meeting those needs with someone else. The lust of the flesh and the lust of the eyes win the day.

While there are relational needs met in marriage, God is the primary source when it comes to our needs. That sounds like Christian cliché, but it is critical for Christians to understand that they don't have to go around God for what they are looking for in their lives. That is exactly what takes place in adultery. This isn't meeting my needs, but that over there would. In his book *Married for God: Making Your Marriage the Best It Can Be*, Christopher Ash writes about some of the problematic approaches found in contemporary marriage advice and resources: "Inside marriage we often talk about how to communicate better, how to be more intimate, how to have better sex, how to be happy. If a marriage isn't serving God, no amount of personal and sexual fulfillment will make it right."[5]

As a pastor, I have counseled far too many couples through affairs and cared for those who have endured the pain of discovering that their spouse was unfaithful. In every single one of these instances, I can confidently say that those who committed adultery were not walking with Christ at the time. Rather, they were going to church occasionally, living their life in secret with a forbidden person throughout the week, and then coming home to put the kids in bed, say prayers, and sleep next to their spouses like everything was normal. Or they were experiencing serious delusions about what God wanted for them. But the secrecy of their actions reveals that they could intuit that their behavior was not sanctioned. It is textbook hypocrisy. It is a spiritual problem before it is a marriage problem. It's forgetting the obvious: that even if no one else knows,

God already does. In the proverb warning of adultery, we are reminded clearly: "For a man's ways are before the LORD's eyes, and he considers all his paths" (Prov. 5:21). The writer reminds the adulterous man that while nobody else may know of his sin—his double life—God knows. But due to sin's deception, the guilty party usually doesn't care. Until a fallout comes.

"Why, my son, would you lose yourself with a forbidden woman or embrace a wayward woman?" (Prov. 5:20). How could one be willing to throw away his or her family, integrity, reputation in the community, and ultimately his or her relationship with God simply for a sexual encounter or a relationship? Often people cannot answer this question. They might point to a lack of intimacy at home or blame the stress of life or work, claiming to need some sort of escape, but the true answer is a spiritual one. They never thought they would get caught, and they loved the thrill of the attraction, the attention, and the high of the forbidden activity. There is something enticing about sin, and this dates back to the garden of Eden. In the fall of man, we believed the lie that God's rules meant missing out on true fulfillment. There is a reason why Proverbs 5 tells us that the "lips of the forbidden woman drip honey" (v. 3). Sin often looks so alluring and enticing, but it cannot and will not satisfy, because "the wages of sin is death" (Rom. 6:23) and life apart from God is no life at all.

When I step into a counseling session with a couple, one of the first questions I ask is whether there has been an affair. The answer to that question lets me know exactly what I'm dealing with. If the couple is coming to see me to discuss issues with parenting, in-laws, finances, or communication, I know our sessions won't be very complicated, and some simple changes in their way of doing things as a couple can bring about a healthy change in the dynamics of their home. But when I find out there was an affair, I take a deep breath, knowing some serious counseling is coming from a licensed marriage therapist, because the hurt is so deep and often the pain is too much to overcome. Adultery is the ultimate act of betrayal against another human. It is the breaking of a covenant. While forgiveness is certainly a Christian command and should be given to anyone who has committed adultery and repented, it is often truly difficult to save a marriage after an affair. I've seen it done, and God is good, but Scripture's allowance of a divorce by the victim of infidelity speaks to God's understanding of the pain adultery inflicts. In our efforts to patch the union together, we can't minimize the reality of what has taken place. When we disregard God's design, brokenness is the result.

Proverbs makes clear what will be the future of the adulterer as a result of his choices:

> A wicked man's iniquities will trap him;
> he will become tangled in the ropes of his own sin.
> He will die because there is no discipline
> and be lost because of his great stupidity. (Prov. 5:22–23)

It is important to note that while the proverb doesn't mince any words describing the forbidden woman tempting the married man to a sexual affair, it also doesn't blame her. It is the iniquities of the man and his "great stupidity" and lack of discipline that trap him. He is the one who failed to enjoy the wife of his youth. Likewise, neither does the spouse who has been cheated on bear responsibility.

Thankfully, there is hope for the adulterer. Thanks to Christ, where sin multiplied, grace multiplied even more (Rom. 5:20). In John's Gospel, we find the famous story of a woman caught in adultery being brought before Jesus by the scribes and Pharisees:[6]

> Then the scribes and the Pharisees brought a woman caught
> in adultery, making her stand in the center. "Teacher," they

said to him, "this woman was caught in the act of committing adultery. In the law Moses commanded us to stone such
women. So what do you say?" They asked this to trap him, in
order that they might have evidence to accuse him.

Jesus stooped down and started writing on the ground
with his finger. When they persisted in questioning him, he
stood up and said to them, "The one without sin among you
should be the first to throw a stone at her." Then he stooped
down again and continued writing on the ground. When they
heard this, they left one by one, starting with the older men.
Only he was left, with the woman in the center. When Jesus
stood up, he said to her, "Woman, where are they? Has no one
condemned you?"

"No one, Lord," she answered.

"Neither do I condemn you," said Jesus. "Go, and from now
on do not sin anymore." (John 8:3–11)

The ones who wanted to condemn her, couldn't. The One who
could have condemned her, wouldn't. Such is the grace of God.

While some might not be able to repair their marriages after
an adulterous affair (even though there are many stories of couples healing and reconciling, by God's grace), their fellowship
with Christ and the church can certainly be restored, since we are
promised that "if we confess our sins, he is faithful and righteous
to forgive us our sins and to cleanse us from all unrighteousness"
(1 John 1:9). One thing we must maintain is that adultery is not
the will of God for any person, and there's no justification for it
being permissible.

Physical adultery stems from spiritual adultery. Remaining
faithful to the Lord will result in remaining faithful to one's spouse.
If we remain faithful to the one who is our bridegroom, marital
faithfulness on earth will be one of many fruits of the spiritual,

heavenly marriage of Christ and the church. While the adulterous woman's lips drip with honey, there is a better tasting honey God offers His people—one that lasts; one that is good. It is the honey that comes from the wisdom found in God's Word and from doing things by God's design:

Eat honey, my son, for it is good,
and the honeycomb is sweet to your palate;
realize that wisdom is the same for you.
If you find it, you will have a future,
and your hope will never fade. (Prov. 24:13–14)

10

LIE NO. 7:
"Cohabitation Just
Makes Sense"

W here are you going on your honeymoon, your bedroom?"
That's what a friend of mine said to his adult daughter when she got engaged after five years of cohabiting with her boyfriend. Even once engaged, she had no wedding date in sight. When you already have many of the benefits of marriage without the commitment, what's the rush? Unmarried couples living together is absolutely the new status quo in America. Cohabitation is the state of living together and having a sexual relationship without being married.[1] Functionally, it lies somewhere between the new version of an exclusive relationship and the new engagement. Cohabitation presents a faux commitment. It is an arrangement to live together for as long as it works.

As a pastor, I am regularly asked to officiate wedding ceremonies. You would be surprised at how many nominally Christian couples are living together but still want me to read Scripture, pray, and give a short sermon during the ceremony, as if they have no idea that they are walking in stark contrast to the ethic of the belief system they claim. The inconsistency between what the couple wants the ceremony to entail and the current sinful lifestyle they are living in does not even seem to cross their minds.

A Pew Research Center study[2] showed that white Evangelical Protestants and black Protestants are the religious groups least likely to say that it's acceptable for an unmarried couple to live together even if they don't plan to get married. However, more than one-in-three white Evangelicals and almost half of black Protestants believe cohabiting is acceptable. Seventy-four percent of Catholics have no issue with a couple living together before marriage. And, since the 1960s, the percentage of men and women who live together before marriage has jumped by almost 900 percent.[3]

I believe two things have contributed to this rapid increase. Both fall under the umbrella of contemporary marriage being understood as a capstone rather than a cornerstone. The first is simply that the sexual revolution has absorbed cultural Christianity, but not to the point where all basic principles are fully renounced. In other words, in a world where anything goes, being exclusive to one partner of the opposite sex might seem like a conservative lifestyle, so people can deceive themselves into believing that cohabitation is not in conflict with Christian beliefs. Many may have been raised by other nominal Christians and therefore have never come into contact with a biblical sexual ethic. For the average cultural Christian, conflict over cohabitation is not "a thing." There's often no pushback from his or her nominal Christian friends, and no one from a local church knows him or her enough to have functional influence or authority to address it. The sexual revolution has influenced the cohabitating couple by presenting any pushback to sex before marriage as outdated and, most significantly, unrealistic. Even if one or both sets of parents aren't thrilled with the idea, chances are they don't want to say anything to disturb relational peace. Instead, they just hope the couple gets married soon. In the cohabiting couple's minds, living together while unmarried is just what you do.

The other factor is that people have adopted the world's wisdom, to which cohabitation and premarital sex simply "makes sense." In my far-too-frequent conversations with engaged couples who are cohabiting and want me to officiate their wedding, addressing the topic of them living together as unmarried people results in them looking at me like I'm crazy. Why would they not live together? In their eyes it makes relational sense (as a type of trial period to see how they exist together under the same roof, whether they are sexually compatible, etc.) and financial sense (as an alternative to having two separate leases, utility bills, etc.). From a worldly perspective, since they are going to eventually get married one of these days, this makes perfect sense.

But Paul wrote to the Corinthians (who were entrenched in sexual sin, among other things) that God's foolishness is wiser than human wisdom (1 Cor. 1:25). People who claim the name of Christ must accept the reality that God's wisdom was never designed to make sense to a sinful world. It is and has always been a countercultural wisdom. An unmarried couple wanting to follow Jesus and live faithfully as God's people should be willing to make the decision, however inconvenient it feels at the time, to live in two different locations until they are married. In the local church where I serve as a pastor, I have seen families open their homes, rent-free, to give a spare bedroom to an engaged person who wants to faithfully live for Christ during engagement but also doesn't want to take out a separate lease. If a local church community desires to see faithfulness in this area, generous hospitality is part of the equation. The family of God should be willing to step up to the plate to eliminate financial roadblocks (or excuses) that would lead members of the church to live in sin by cohabiting. I have heard of a church that agreed to pay one of the two leases if one party of an engaged couple would agree to move out and if the couple committed to sexual purity until their wedding day.

Or (parents, plug your ears), if you're an engaged Christian and you're tempted concerning sexual immorality, move your wedding date up or get married immediately and then have a party later—don't drag it out for reasons like flowers or venue timelines. When an engaged couple who is cohabiting gives the world's list of reasons for why they are choosing to live together, I usually encourage them that the easiest remedy for everything they are stating might be to just go ahead and get married earlier or even as soon as possible, which could mean heading down to the courthouse that afternoon. This sounds like the dumbest idea ever if one believes the wisdom of the world, especially when a couple has put down a non-refundable deposit for a wedding venue at a date fourteen months from now. But Jesus commands us to obey now, not later when it's convenient.

A couple I know named Anna and Mark[4] met and started dating while college students and got engaged shortly before their graduation. Upon graduation, Mark landed a dream job in another state and had two weeks to relocate, while Anna was planning to move home with her parents until the wedding, which was about eight months away. After realizing that long-distance wasn't what they wanted, Anna decided to move to where Mark was living and get a job so they wouldn't have to spend the rest of their engagement apart. Mark and Anna were church members in good standing and committed to following Christ. When I got word that Anna was moving to where Mark had just relocated, I was excited for them and glad to hear the news. But after a month or so had passed, I had a thought when I saw a picture of them together enjoying their new city on social media. "Wait a second," I thought, "It's still several months away from their marriage, and Anna moved out there on a whim. I hope they aren't living together." Having the relational clout to ask, I called Anna, who I knew the best out of the two. After catching up for a couple minutes, I asked her, "did you get your own place to live?"

Anna paused, and then nervously brought up how hard and expensive it would have been to find a short lease. She also acknowledged that they knew it was wrong and were going to try their best not to give into temptation. Since they were getting married in several months, she reasoned, it would be so much easier to just live in the place Mark had already moved into. My reply was sincere and direct. Well-aware that Anna knew better than this, I simply asked, "Anna, what are you doing?" Frustrated, she told me she didn't have any other options.

I understood her dilemma. Moving to a new city a few months before her wedding and not wanting to take on the expense of a lease in a large city, especially when she hadn't even started her new job yet, was obviously complicated. Yes, she could have stayed home with her family until the wedding, but she was now there in her new city, with Mark, about to start a new job. I told Anna I understood the complexity of it all but that there was an alternative that I believed would honor the Lord and protect the integrity of the Christian witness she and Mark possessed. "Anna," I said, "get married tomorrow." She laughed and told me I was crazy. "My mom would practically disown me! I can't get married without my parents here, and they've already paid for a wedding." I encouraged her that she could still have her wedding on the original date and see it as a public celebration of what they could do at the courthouse or with a notary, tomorrow. As the one scheduled to officiate their planned wedding, I offered to jump on a plane and be the one to marry them now. I asked her what was more important, her mom's approval or God's approval. Flustered, she got off the phone, not wanting to discuss it anymore.

The next day, I got a text from Anna with a picture of her and Mark standing in front of the courthouse, holding a marriage license. The accompanying text read, "my mom is mad at you." It gave me a good laugh. Mark and Anna showed what it looked like to choose Christ over the wisdom of the world. I was so proud of their decision and had the chance to be part of their celebration several months later, where they asked me to explain their reasoning for choosing to get married months before their actual wedding. More than a decade later, they are a growing family with children, involved in their local church and living for Christ in the same city where they walked to the courthouse and chose to build their lives by God's design rather than live in a quasi-marriage based on convenience. Following Jesus interferes with one's life, even when—by the world's wisdom—it makes little sense. David Shuman summarizes this decision well: "When we wait to live together until we're married, it demonstrates that Christ is our King, and that what he says matters to us."[5]

Many cohabiting couples identify as Christians and nonetheless ask a pastor, not a notary, to officiate the wedding. The religious component is important for the wedding but not the relationship. Only fourteen percent of Americans say cohabitation is never acceptable, and "most Americans (69%) say cohabitation is acceptable even if the couple doesn't plan to get married."[6] Yet a 2019 Pew Research Center survey indicated that 70.6% of Americans claim to be Christians.[7] That seems like some fuzzy math. There are only three explanations for this massive discrepancy:

- Many professing Christians are ignorant of biblical sexual ethics.
- Many professing Christians are directly disobeying what the Bible says regarding sex or don't believe it really applies.
- Many professing Christians are not actually Christians.

There is probably a mix of the three, but I believe the primary contributor is cultural Christianity, meaning people who ascribe to a generic theism and the warm fuzzies of religion but are not actually Christians by conviction. Following Jesus is not a primary component of cultural Christianity. Vague moral values du jour, yes. Submitting to biblical teachings, no. The keys to addressing the cohabitation crisis among professing Christians, then, are evangelism and discipleship: evangelism first, as many of these people are simply lost and without Christ, and then discipleship that emphasizes biblical literacy and refuses to avoid the Bible's teaching on sexual immorality.

I believe much of the church's pushback against cohabitation uses the wrong approach. This approach has largely focused on using statistics to warn people that cohabitation reduces the likelihood of longevity in marriage, such as well-intentioned arguments like, "Cohabitation rarely leads to 'happily ever after.' 40 percent of people who cohabit break up before marriage. Of those who make it to the altar, couples who live together are almost twice as likely to divorce as compared to those couples who don't live together before marriage."[8]

But this practical information can neither save the lost nor pull the believer to repentance. While knowing those statistics is helpful, the problem remains that no cohabiting couple thinks that is going to be them. I have never heard of someone repenting of sin due to data not being in his or her favor. This is a heart issue which needs to be confronted biblically. Local churches (who can assume that at least some in their congregations are believers) must be unafraid to talk about the cultural phenomenon of cohabitation from the pulpit. They must exercise love and courage to have difficult conversations with people who profess the name of Christ and are part of the local church community and who have chosen cohabitation. A couple must see where their choices are misaligned with their claimed convictions and be confronted with choosing between following Christ in holiness or following the world. Far too often, churches or individual Christians remain silent on this issue or let it go unchallenged under the watch of the leadership. But the apostle Paul writes with clear and firm authority:

> I wrote to you in a letter not to associate with sexually immoral people. I did not mean the immoral people of this world or the greedy and swindlers or idolaters; otherwise you would have to leave the world. But actually, I wrote you not to associate with anyone who claims to be a brother or sister and is sexually immoral or greedy, an idolater or verbally abusive, a drunkard or a swindler. Do not even eat with such a person. For what business is it of mine to judge outsiders? Don't you judge those who are inside? God judges outsiders. Remove the evil person from among you. (1 Cor. 5:9–13)

Paul takes the Christian's relationship with Jesus so seriously that he is willing to disassociate with fellow believers living in sin so that they can begin to comprehend the seriousness of their actions. He also makes it clear that he is not referring to unbelievers. Cohabiting unbelievers need Jesus, much more than they need to live separately in two different apartments. Our concern is much more for their souls than their actions, and putting them under any condemnation or judgment for cohabiting suggests that their issue is cohabiting rather than the need to believe the gospel and trust in Christ. Gospel confusion abounds when we expect people who aren't Christians to think and live like Christians. Paul makes that clear. If Mark and Anna were not Christians, I wouldn't have said a word about their situation. But since I knew they loved Jesus, and I loved them, I had to say something. When it comes to cultural Christians, I think there is a fantastic evangelism opportunity to help them see the disconnect between the faith they claim and the current life they are choosing. There is a good chance they are ignorant concerning the teachings of the Scriptures and have never actually given their lives to Christ.

The goal of addressing cohabitation is not to place rules or burdens upon people but rather to see people flourish in their relationships with Christ as they pursue God's design for their families, which is for the sexual couple to be committed to lifelong marriage. Perhaps one of the greatest examples of what it looks like to "pick up your cross" in the twenty-first century Western world is for Christians to refuse to seek the benefits of marriage without the commitment of marriage. By picking up that cross, they will come to realize that the One who created marriage is the One who knows what is for our good. For those not given the gift of singleness, God's design is marriage, then sex, and building a life together for His glory.

SECTION

Where Do We Go
From Here?

11

TO THE WAITING:
Singleness and
the Gospel

*Then the LORD God said, "It is not good for the man to be alone.
I will make a helper corresponding to him."*

GENESIS 2:18

*I don't say this out of need, for I have learned to be content
in whatever circumstances I find myself.*

PHILIPPIANS 4:11

M uch of this book is about the tension between holding to biblical convictions and rejecting pitfalls of various movements like purity culture. In other words, it is about throwing out the bad from such movements while refusing to throw out the biblical truths that inspired them. One example of this tension is being unapologetic about God's design for marriage without misguiding or mishandling the feelings of single people in the church.

If you're single and involved in the local church, chances are you've been told to "be content." I can imagine that seeming like a cop-out substitute for godly counsel on marriage and sexuality. Sometimes the message single people hear is, "Hey singles, God wants you to be content, and you have so much free time since you aren't married, so get to work at church!" Versions of that argument are encountered in church talks to single people as frequently as one is told that the McDonald's ice cream machine "isn't working right now." It is usually a quick little mention during a sermon on marriage, a cover-your-bases move to "not forget the single people."

Traditionally, churches transition congregants into the singles Sunday school class after college, where you have a forty-three-year-old divorced guy and a twenty-two-year-old girl who hoped she would be engaged by the time of her recent college graduation together in the same class. Neither of them feel great about it, and it is a little awkward, but it is what it is. A church may even have a singles pastor, whose job is to keep you busy so you don't feel as though the church only caters to families. Some churches have now tried to make singles ministry a little more enticing by naming it the "young professionals" class, but it's still unclear exactly who qualifies for that title or when you move on to not-so-young professional status. Somehow, that forty-three-year-old is still in the class, believing that if Tom Brady can win a Super Bowl at forty-three, maybe he just hasn't had his opportunity to thrive yet.

But as is the trend in American Christianity, we love to overcorrect. Nowadays, there is no shortage of blog posts with titles like "5 things to remember as a single Christian" or "7 things the unmarried people in your church wish you knew." Christian singleness has practically become its own industry. Pastors walk on eggshells when talking about marriage and sex, dreading the forthcoming comments that their sermon "didn't apply to single people" and that "the church only seems to focus on families." As a result, there is pressure to feel like an apology is needed when a church focuses on marriage. But the reality is that marriage is a good and grand design. It's not the only status in life God blesses, but it is His idea and we should not apologize for it. Marriage should be supported, taught about, and honored in and by the church.

Notice what I did not say. I did not say that singleness should not be supported, taught about, or honored in the church. Married people are not superior to single people in God's eyes. Jesus and Paul would be in quite the quandary and our Christology would be thrown out the window if singleness were inferior. But that doesn't change the fact that marriage was present at Creation. It was God's intention for His created people before the Fall. The first command ever given by God to humans was one regarding family: to be fruitful and multiply (Gen. 1:28). Marriage and family were and still are God's design. God Himself said that it is not good for man to be alone (Gen. 2:18). A person is no less human if he or she is unmarried, and marriage is certainly not ultimate, as Jesus Himself tells us marriage will not exist in heaven (Luke 20:34–36). However, marriage should be upheld as a good thing for most Christians to pursue. There are exceptions, and Paul isn't afraid to discuss them in 1 Corinthians 7, so I argue that rather than walk on eggshells when it comes to speaking to the unmarried in the church, we ought to speak where the Bible speaks.

Let's look at some of the qualifiers Paul gives for when singleness is the appropriate path instead of marriage. Paul wrote to the Corinthian church, "I wish that all people were as I am [unmarried]. But each has his own gift from God, one person has this gift, another has that" (1 Cor. 7:7). We see here that some people are given the gift of singleness. Paul didn't have to deal

> But both faithful marriage and faithful singleness are countercultural.

with the angry Valentine's Day Christian Twitter mob and wasn't afraid to say exactly what is true regarding singleness: it can be a gift for the kingdom of God. He continues:

> I want you to be without concerns. The unmarried man is concerned about the things of the Lord—how he may please the Lord. But the married man is concerned about the things of the world—how he may please his wife—and his interests are divided. The unmarried woman or virgin is concerned about the things of the Lord, so that she may be holy both in body and in spirit. But the married woman is concerned about the things of the world—how she may please her husband. I am saying this for your own benefit, not to put a restraint on you, but to promote what is proper and so that you may be devoted to the Lord without distraction. (vv. 32–35)

Paul is not shrugging his shoulders, telling single people that because they have more time on their hands, they should be the ones doing all the serving in the church while married people get a pass. The word he speaks to the unmarried is that unlike a married person, their interests aren't divided. The marriage they can solely focus on is that of Christ and the church. Today, such a statement sounds cheesy, like a type of "Jesus is my boyfriend" campaign, and there lies part of the problem of teaching and living in God's design in the twenty-first century church: we are often embarrassed by that design. But both faithful marriage and faithful singleness are countercultural. Nowhere in the Bible do we have a promise from God that living as a sojourner is easy. Instead, we are told that, in Jesus, the yoke is easy and burden is light (Matt. 11:30). Whether called to singleness or to marriage, we can cast our burdens on Him who cares for us (1 Peter 5:7).

I have too many conversations with single people who have

simply given up, now considering sexual purity as either outdated or unrealistic. Katelyn Beaty wrote, "Somehow God and I got our wires crossed, because the husband hasn't arrived. Twenty years later, I no longer subscribe to purity culture, largely because it never had anything to say to Christians past the age of 23."[1] I don't think it matters what purity culture has to say to people past the age of 23, because God is not the author of purity culture. He is the creator of sex, and He certainly has something to say to people from puberty to the grave about what He has made. If our wires get crossed with God, we are the ones who need rewiring. Beaty does understand that the world's sexual ethic is not the alternative to purity culture: "Purity culture as it was modeled for evangelical teenagers in the 1990s is not the future of Christian sexual ethics. But neither is the progressive Christian approach that simply baptizes casual sex in the name of self-expression and divorces sex from covenant faithfulness and self-sacrificial love."[2] In the midst of these two competing mindsets toward sex, I believe God has something to say to unmarried adults who lived in the purity culture era. Tactics and trends change; God doesn't. His design doesn't change because young professionals in big cities find it unreasonable and unrealistic. There isn't a waiver that God hands out that allows you to become one flesh with someone other than your spouse once you've reached a certain age.

But singleness isn't all burden and no joy. A single person can uniquely display part of the gospel story in their lives, which is certainly a gift for the church. Sam Allberry, an unmarried minister, gives an expression of his personal testimony and gift of singleness when he wrote that "both marriage and singleness point to the gospel: the former reflects its shape, the latter its sufficiency."[3] What a statement. Single adults in the church are not removed from the opportunity and responsibility to reflect the story of the gospel in their lives. Matt Smethurst writes,

"History's most complete person never had sex and never got married. If singleness is deficient, then so was Jesus Christ."[4] Remember that the next time your aunt asks you at Thanksgiving why you aren't married yet. Being single should not put someone on the defensive, as often seems to be the norm in Christian culture.

Another exception Paul brings to the table is life circumstances during which it might be unwise to get married and start a family. He gives his opinion for the Corinthian believers by stating, "Now about virgins: I have no command from the Lord, but I do give an opinion as one who by the Lord's mercy is faithful. Because of the present distress, I think that it is good for a man to remain as he is" (1 Cor. 7:25–26). Some scholars believe that there was persecution taking place at the time that endangered Christian men especially. As a result, marriage might not have been the best idea for Paul's original audience. As a parallel example in our modern culture, when marriage isn't an option, one could justify a charge to "kiss dating goodbye." Entering a serious dating relationship when marriage is not possible, or even not best, is simultaneously unwise and unloving. It is unwise due to sexual temptation that persists in dating relationships that are simply for the sake of dating, and it is unloving to place another person in such a relationship that has no actual destination in sight. If you believe that marriage is currently not an option, then dating is also not an option for that given season. Your life might not be at risk, but if marriage or "settling down" isn't currently on your agenda, dating shouldn't be either. Friendship makes much more sense in this scenario, especially for believers wanting to walk in purity.

However, most Christian singles (at least most of the ones I know) aren't single because they see singleness as a gift or because their current circumstances make marriage unwise, but rather because they haven't met someone to date or someone they want to keep dating. This is where the contentment conversation must come into focus. I see this being an increasing reality for Christian women due to the growing disparity between the numbers of Christian men and women in the church. It is easy for a Christian woman to look around her church and ask, "Where are the men?" This is a matter of urgency for churches in general, as men are slipping away from the local church and creating generational patterns for the future. Men are by and large not giving their lives to Jesus, and there are far too many who profess to be Christians but are not being discipled in a local church context. Women not only make up a greater percentage of the American Christian population than men,[5] but Christian women are also more likely than Christian men to say that they believe in God with absolute certainty,[6] that their faith is important to them,[7] that they pray at least daily,[8] and that they regularly attend religious services.[9] The result is that there are fewer eligible singles for serious Christians. It really is that simple. Many Christians are not interested in dating someone who isn't serious about Christ. Finding a new church is not the answer because this problem stretches to most churches, and one does not leave a church where he or she is committed only for the purpose of finding a spouse. Contentment, in prayer, is the only option for the serious believer.

The conversation around contentment in singleness is complicated because it can be interpreted to suggest that the desire to be married is some type of affront on being content as a single person. However, one can believe that "it is not good for man to be alone" while still learning to be content in his or her life situation. Those two are not at odds with each other. Contentment is so difficult to achieve in any area of life that Paul claimed it is only possible through the strength of Christ (Phil. 4:13). On his own, he had no chance. Church leadership will do a great service to all people in the congregation if the topic of contentment is frequently visited and mentioned in prayer and seen as a Christian virtue rather than a consolation prize. One can look for a spouse and feel unashamed for being on the search. In doing so, you are pursuing God's design.

The opposite of contentment is resentment. Human nature can turn a bridesmaid invitation or a social media post about another college frat brother's engagement into a personal affront, causing a person to wonder, "Why them and not me?" That may be a rational response, but it is not a righteous response. A clear indication that one is struggling with resentment and bitterness is the inability to be happy for someone else. A single person in a church setting is vulnerable if seeing others get engaged, married, or pregnant drums up resentment. The apostle Paul would declare boldly that in Christ, resentment can be fought. This is not a Sunday school answer; it is his sincere hope as someone who "learned to be content in whatever circumstances" (Phil. 4:11). Paul claimed he now knew "how to make do with little, and I know how to make do with a lot. In any and all circumstances I have learned the secret of being content—whether well fed or hungry, whether in abundance or in need" (v. 12).

There was nothing sinful about Paul wanting to be well fed. I am sure most of us would rather not be "in need." But in Christ, he could be content regardless of his circumstances. Through Christ who gave him strength, Paul found the secret to contentment: believing Jesus is the greatest blessing in life. For singles in the church, there must be a similar focus on contentment through Christ as an alternative to either joining the sexual ethics of the world or seeing singleness as merely a waiting period until actual flourishing takes place.

In conclusion, I want to address three things that need to be made clear concerning singles in the church.

1. MARRIAGE DOES NOT EQUAL HAPPINESS, BUT IT'S OKAY TO ADMIT THAT SINGLENESS IS HARD.

Far too often, the church's word to single adults is that Prince Charming is going to come sweep you off your feet or Rapunzel is going to let down her hair, and once that happens, you will finally be happy. While God said it is good for man not to be alone, that does not insinuate that everyone who is unmarried is not good. A person can be single and not alone. We are not meant to be isolated, but in community. And God has designed the local church as the beautiful and fulfilling context in which we can experience true community. Plenty of single adult Christians are thriving in community because they are part of a local church.

However, with every path of sanctification, there is difficulty. Vaughan Roberts writes that while "the New Testament is positive about singleness, there's no doubt marriage is regarded as the norm. It is God's loving gift to humanity and the chief context in which our desire for intimacy is met. Single people are therefore likely to struggle with loneliness and sexual temptation. Those struggles are certainly not exclusive to the unmarried, but they are very much a part of the single condition."[10] Loneliness and temptation are only made worse by the aggressive sexual agenda of the surrounding world. Even twenty and thirty years ago, popular sitcoms like Seinfeld and Friends normalized casual sex with strangers. Characters like Rachel and Monica glamorized the single life by framing it as a free pursuit of sex. It's even been said that celibacy is the only known sexual perversion.[11]

That messaging can make it difficult to be a single person who believes in God's design for marriage and physical intimacy. I am not saying that single Christians simply want to have sex and therefore are going to adopt the mantra, "If you can't beat them, join them," regarding the world's sexual ethic. Rather, we must acknowledge that the dating culture that exists today is one where sex is expected. Moreover, some thirty-year-old single Christians might correctly and fairly assert that their peer who got married at twenty-two doesn't understand what it's like to live alone through your twenties. So we as members of the family of Christ must be cognizant of our shared call to purity and of its different logistical outworkings.

While secular marriage and Christian marriage can mirror each other in certain ways (for example, no one likes to be cheated on), singleness is different. The single life of a Christian should be so foreign to the single life of the world that it is unrecognizable. Churches must acknowledge that while the unmarried life of the world is glamorized, the single life of a follower of Jesus is a stark contrast to what we stream on our TVs.

Lonely people should not exist in the family of God. In the same way that isolation in marriage can lead to a lack of flourishing, the same is true for the unmarried. There is so much pressure to appear strong and independent—not "needing" someone—that it can cause a lack of transparency in conversations with church family. Instead, let our churches be places where we bear the "one another" commands of Scripture.

2. SINGLENESS IS NOT A SECOND-CLASS STATUS.

How often has a single adult been told, "I can't believe you're still single; what are these guys/girls out there thinking?" The statement assumes that there is something wrong with the single status and that Prince Charming simply needs to get a clue and rectify the situation. Christians often treat weddings as a graduation ceremony, promotion, or acceptance onto some varsity team. How drastic the disconnect between those connotations and Scripture, where Paul calls singleness a gift. Robert Mounce notes that throughout Scripture, God compares the true, pure church to a virgin devoted to God, as in Revelation 14:4: "They are virgins who have not defiled themselves with women; they are followers of the Lamb; and they are firstfruits purchased from among men."[12] Unmarried Christians are not to feel benched from meaningful life. Quite the contrary! They can "follow the Lamb wherever He goes." Brooks Waldron rightly responds to this observation by stating, "Through the single person's commitment to follow Christ 'wherever he goes,' especially through the suffering of refraining from marital and sexual intimacy, the commitment to Christ that the whole church is called to is clearly illustrated."[13] Singleness is hardly a lesser status or the junior varsity of the Christian life. Single Christians struggling with their present state must walk the sanctification process of agreeing with the Scriptures regarding the value of being single. Otherwise contentment will remain in the category of Sunday school answers rather than part of the biblical path toward a life that pleases God.

3. YOU MIGHT NOT EVER GET MARRIED.

I remember hearing an illustration during a talk on dating and marriage when I was in college. The speaker said that if you are looking figuratively up to the sky, focusing on the Lord, then you will bump into the person of the opposite sex who is doing the same. "Focus on God, not on finding someone, and then you'll meet the perfect person." It's no wonder there is so much annoyance and frustration when it comes to the topics of marriage and sexuality. Such a mindset also creates unrealistic standards for those who do get married. "Focus on Jesus and it will all work out!" Says who? And does "it will all work out" simply mean marriage?

We need to be careful not to make promises to people that God never made. Otherwise people will be left wondering if they looked to Jesus with enough focus, or if, in the name of a subtle prosperity gospel, they did something wrong, and God is withholding a spouse as a result.

For the person who wants to be married but realizes that a life of celibacy is a potential reality, Paul's words will hit close to home:

> The creation eagerly waits with anticipation for God's sons to be revealed. . . .
>
> For we know that the whole creation has been groaning together with labor pains until now. Not only that, but we ourselves who have the Spirit as the firstfruits—we also groan within ourselves, eagerly waiting for adoption, the redemption of our bodies. Now in this hope we were saved, but hope that is seen is not hope, because who hopes for what he sees? Now if we hope for what we do not see, we eagerly wait for it with patience. (Rom. 8:19, 22–25)

Tim Keller comments on this passage of Scripture, stating that, "this is the future—the fulfilling, renewing, joy-giving future—creation can look forward to since it's the future God's children look forward to. This is Paul's answer to the question about whether our future glory makes our present sufferings worth bearing. Even creation, he observes, urges you to say *yes!*"[14] Staying with Jesus, maintaining the faith, and agreeing with God on His design is worth it for the single person who desires to be married but is aware that day might not come. Others may see singleness as a gift, and while they may be open to and even desire marriage, they have no issue with remaining single for their entire lives. This is not a better way than the struggling single per se, but it is one that doesn't feel anguish or sulk. It is important to know that all unmarried Christians do not have the same approach to being single and that the Bible implies that some should remain single and others should pursue marriage (1 Cor. 7:8–9).

While there is not a one-size-fits-all approach to singleness for the Christian, there is one sexual ethic—a design that dates back to creation. Finding contentment in Christ as an unmarried Christian cannot be detached from a convictional belief in God's design. One does not live in contentment by departing from that design, going around God for meaning, acceptance, fulfillment, and love rather than to God Himself. The single life is not a second-class life, and God's sexual ethic is not merely an optional path for those claiming to be His disciples. As Vaughan Roberts summarizes, "For as long as you have it, that is a gift from God, just as marriage will be God's gift if you ever receive it. We should receive our situation in life, whether it is singleness or marriage, as a gift of God's grace to us."[15]

12

God Gives a "Way Out"

One of the most comforting passages of Scripture for my life continues to be 1 Corinthians 10:13. After Paul warns the believers about not letting their guard down regarding temptation, he gives them encouragement in the form of assurance: "No temptation has come upon you except what is common to humanity. But God is faithful; he will not allow you to be tempted beyond what you are able, but with the temptation he will also provide the way out so that you may be able to bear it" (1 Cor. 10:13).

It helps me to remember the truths compiled in that single verse:

- My temptation is not unique. And neither is yours. It is common to humanity.
- God is faithful.
- God will not let us be tempted beyond what we—as regenerate followers of Christ, possessing the Holy Spirit—can reject.
- God will give us a way out when we are tempted.

In a world where the siren's call of temptation is chanting our names minute by minute, Paul's words to the Corinthians give me comfort and hope. In the same letter, Paul spends much time and effort dealing with sexual immorality among the Christians (1 Cor. 5–7). Then, in chapter ten, he assures them that God is with them and has given them a way out.

Sexual sin is not inevitable for those who are in Christ.

When I was in college, Dwayne Carson, the campus pastor of our school, gave us four words to remember when it came to dealing with temptation in our lives. Years later, as I continue to see the story of believers dealing with temptation in the Scriptures, I am more convinced than ever of these four words and have come to call them the "Fab Four" of seeing the "way out" of temptation that God provides. Since the tempter "is prowling around like a roaring lion, looking for anyone he can devour" (1 Peter 5:8), we must do whatever it takes to tap into the great promise of 1 Corinthians 10:13, which God has graciously given His people.

1. FEED

The first step to overcoming temptation is to feed our hearts and minds with the Word of God. Jesus is the ultimate model for us here. When He was genuinely tempted in the wilderness by Satan, rather than failing (like the Hebrew people who failed to trust God in the wilderness), Jesus succeeded. First Corinthians 10:13 is true for us because Jesus refused to bow to the tempter. Jesus "has been tempted in every way as we are, yet without sin" (Heb. 4:15). There were three separate temptations from Satan, and Jesus answered all three by quoting Scripture.

Out of the three, one sticks out to me as especially helpful in dealing with temptations of sexual sin. While that was not the actual temptation Jesus encountered, His answer certainly applies to our topic. "After he had fasted forty days and forty nights, he was hungry. Then the tempter approached him and said, 'If you are the Son of God, tell these stones to become bread.' He answered, 'It is written: Man must not live on bread alone but on every word that comes from the mouth of God'" (Matt. 4:2–4).

Here stood Jesus, hungry (read here, he had a biological appetite or "need"), and Satan was ready to provide Him with a quick fix to His hunger. All He had to do was obey, and bread would be coming His way. There was an issue, however, that was going to cause the devil's biscuits to be rejected by the Son of God. Jesus wasn't about to go around God to meet His desires, because unlike the Hebrews in the wilderness who wanted instant gratification, Jesus did not live by bread alone.

> Remember that the LORD your God led you on the entire journey these forty years in the wilderness, so that he might humble you and test you to know what was in your heart, whether or not you would keep his commands. He humbled you by letting you go hungry; then he gave you manna to eat, which you and your ancestors had not known, so that you might learn that man does not live on bread alone but on every word that comes from the mouth of the LORD. (Deut. 8:2–3)

Our longings and hungers show us that we are desperate and dependent upon God to meet our needs. And time and time again, God shows that He's able and trustworthy to do so. But his faithful provision might not be physically seen or felt in this life. Teaching about how we must hunger and thirst for righteousness, Russell Moore said, "The very fact you have a sense that things aren't what they're supposed to be, that's a sign God has a resolution to that in the age to come."[1]

The Son of God was tested as Israel was tested, hungry as Israel was hungry, but knew that God would meet His need by more than bread—with His very self. John Piper comments on this story, "Every word that comes out of the mouth of God reveals God. And it is this self-revelation that we feed on. This will last forever. This is eternal life. Begone, Satan, God is my portion. I will not turn from his path and his fellowship, not even for miraculous manna."[2] We need to feed ourselves from God's word so that when we are tempted, we remember His goodness and remember that it is when we hunger and thirst for righteousness that we will actually be filled (Matt. 5:6). The food this world has to offer us is like cotton candy—colorful and sweet for a moment but unable to meet any true need.

King David, a man who gave into his sexual desires and committed sexual sin with significant consequences, wrote:

> How can a young man keep his way pure?
> By keeping your word.
> I have sought you with all my heart;
> don't let me wander from your commands.
> I have treasured your word in my heart
> so that I may not sin against you. (Ps. 119:9–11)

David, called a "man after [God's] own heart" (Acts 13:22), knew that his heart would not be pure unless he kept God's Word. He would wander unless he treasured the Word of God in his heart. Lord, help us to hunger and thirst for You!

2. FELLOWSHIP

In a society that has fully embraced the sexual revolution, surrounding oneself with a community of people who share biblical convictions is absolutely critical for Christians. In the book of Acts, we repeatedly see a theme of Christian fellowship—put more plainly as Christians routinely doing things together. United together in fellowship, the "entire group of those who believed were of one heart and mind" (Acts 4:32). In a period of history where those converting to Christianity risked and endured alienation, persecution, and sometimes death, the fellowship of the body of Christ was essential. While physical persecution might not be the current reality for Christians in the modern West, holding to a biblical sexual ethic still places us at odds with the gods of our age. Our culture teaches that the only thing out of bounds is to claim something is out of bounds. So, as you can imagine, there are many people who take serious issue with biblical sexual ethics. Not only do we need like-minded Christians to help us fight assimilation into this culture, but we need each other in general.

> Faithful perseverance for Christ is going to require a commitment to the fellowship of the local church.

I know Christians who have been alienated from their families for not embracing a sibling's same-sex marriage. I regularly talk to believers who have had friends disconnect from them completely due to confrontation over different sexual sins, and I know others who are mocked and ridiculed for holding to biblical convictions in the choices they make in their dating relationships. When it comes to living in this world as "strangers and exiles" (1 Peter 2:11), faithful perseverance for Christ is going to require a commitment to the fellowship of the local church. God has given us the gift of Christian fellowship. What a mistake if we don't cling to the spiritual family He has provided to join us in the quest of the Great Commission in our world.

Being around other people with shared convictions helps you know that you aren't crazy, intolerant, oppressive, or a prude simply based on what you believe about sex. We need to see that we aren't alone. We also need to encourage one another to keep the faith based on a love for God and a love for others. Our fellowship will influence our commitment to living within God's design, because our deepest relationships will be with people who won't tempt us with the world's wisdom. For the unmarried in the church, this is extremely beneficial, as the common approach to dating and friendship with the opposite sex will not be laced with sexual overtones or ungodly expectations. There is a good kind of solidarity among people who know they are living in a world that is not their home and maintain a bond of being unashamed of the Scriptures and committed to walk with one another. Paul instructed the Thessalonian Christians, "Let us be self-controlled and put on the armor of faith and love, and a helmet of the hope of salvation. For God did not appoint us to wrath, but to obtain salvation through our Lord Jesus Christ, who died for us, so that whether we are awake or asleep, we may live together with him. Therefore encourage one another and build each other up as you are already doing" (1 Thess. 5:8–11).

As we aim to live for Christ in this world, we need encouragement from one another, and to build each other up in the faith. It is common to see Christians influenced by the pressures of this world to make cultural accommodations against their convictions in the workplace, and the same temptations are present in a school setting for younger Christians and college students. Yet we need support to hold onto "the faith that was delivered to the saints once for all" (Jude 1:3). Every single time I have seen someone abandon orthodox views on sexuality, it has been the result of either a lifestyle decision or the company that was kept, influencing that person to embrace a contrary worldview. Christian fellowship is essential to keeping the faith.

3. FLEE

God has a clear word for the church when it comes to sexual immorality: "flee" (1 Cor. 6:18). He gives no nuance or gray area concerning the matter. When He tells us that He will give a way out when we are tempted (1 Cor. 10:13), there is one way that is always available, and that is to completely bail out like a fighter pilot hitting the ejection button on a crashing jet. I can think of times in my life when I have committed sins that so easily could have been avoided if I had just left the scene.

The account of Joseph and Potiphar's wife from the book of Genesis is often held up as the model for this, and rightfully so. When Potiphar's wife propositioned Joseph, he literally fled. I imagine him sprinting out the door like an Olympic runner off the starting block. Perhaps Joseph knew he was weak and vulnerable in the face of temptation, or maybe he was terrified of Potiphar walking in the door, but regardless, when he had the opportunity for sexual sin, he fled the scene. I believe it is because Joseph was well aware that His sovereign God would know, and that was enough reason to flee. Aware of my sinful nature, I should refuse to rely on my own strength, especially when God gives me a clear opportunity to run out the door. The longer I linger, the more I expose myself to the lion who prowls.

My favorite Christian band growing up was a group named Caedmon's Call. They have a song titled "Potiphar's Door" that helps bring the story of Joseph to life in relation to the temptations believers find themselves facing. One lyric has stuck in my mind for years, even decades after the song was written: "So I'm knocking on Potiphar's door sayin' 'Hey, on second thought, I might be in for some more.'"[3] How often is that our situation when we are tempted? The mental battle, the reconsidering, thinking that maybe it isn't that big of a deal or that it will only be one time—

the only solution is to flee. Rather than knock on that door that leads to death, we must run away into life.

4. FIGHT

There are times, hopefully rare, when we must declare an absolute internal war on the flesh and fight for holiness. I think of Paul's battle in Romans 7, where he says he knows what to do but struggles to do it. Sometimes knowing Bible verses, having strong relationships, and even the opportunity to flee are not helping in the moment, and we must fight. Paul reminds the Ephesians that "our struggle is not against flesh and blood, but against the rulers, against the authorities, against the cosmic powers of this darkness, against evil, spiritual forces in the heavens" (Eph. 6:12). Knowing that God ultimately wins the battle against Satan is our assurance that the battle belongs to the Lord. He is with us and calls us to put on His armor and fight (Eph. 6:11).

I coach a middle school football team, and we regularly line up to play against teams that are bigger and faster. I tell my team before those games that we are going to have to fight. I don't mean a physical altercation where punches are being thrown, but an attitude that understands this is going to be a battle. A great question for Christians regarding sexual sin is, "Are you willing to declare war and fight?" Let us not for a moment believe that suggesting such measures is extremism or legalism. It is the devil who is extreme, wanting us to conform to the legalism of his rules which hurl us into the false promises of the sexual revolution. Our enemy wants us to believe that freedom and flourishing are found anywhere but in the design and will of our Creator. We must fight for the fidelity of our marriages, for our commitment to sexual purity, for victory over pornography, and make every effort to resist the temptation to pledge allegiance to the gods of this world.

Our victory is in Christ. He does not lose. May we cling to Him and ask for His help to war against the darkness. May we "walk by the Spirit and . . . not carry out the desire of the flesh" (Gal. 5:16).

13

What I Wish The True Love Waits Movement Would Have Taught Me

It doesn't get more biblical than claiming that God has designed sex to be enjoyed exclusively between a man and a woman who are husband and wife. That's not "purity culture," that's Bible. Thus, a culture of purity should be seen as a conviction toward godliness, not shame. True godliness does not come in the form of pharisaical legalism. Jesus had constant tension throughout the Gospels with the Pharisees and scribes of His day, claiming they would "tie up heavy loads that are hard to carry and put them on people's shoulders" (Matt. 23:4). Jesus offered Himself as the incredible alternative: "For my yoke is easy and my burden is light" (Matt. 11:30). Jesus was not suggesting that following Him was an easy task, but He Himself is not a burden. The True Love Waits message of purity culture unintentionally placed a heavy burden upon a generation of young people in two primary ways: first, by misplacing the primary motivation for sexual purity onto a future spouse instead of on God, and second, by insinuating that those who had committed sexual sin had become second-class citizens.

When I preach sermons on sexual immorality to an audience of students or single adults, I never mention a future spouse as the motivation for sexual purity. Rather, I present God's design for sexuality and show that it is for His glory and for our good. I wish True Love Waits and purity culture had made the pursuit of purity about pursuing Christ. There are four primary things I wish the movement would have taught us. And, in true pastor fashion, I'm about to use some alliteration.

1. THE REASON

A theology of sex is first and foremost about the glory of God. At the True Love Waits rallies I attended as a middle and high school student, the reason for not having sex before marriage was never presented in the context of God's glory or His design. It was preached to us as a rule not to mess up. God certainly has rules, and Christians should not apologize for them. Our holy God has every right to tell His people to "do this and not that." But rather than function exclusively as a judge, God speaks as a father to His children. God's rules are never disconnected from His purposes. In other words, God is not on a power trip, throwing out rules for the sake of rules. He knows what we need, and His heart is completely good. How I wish that the glory of God and His design was the way I came to understand a biblical theology of sex.

As a teenager, an emphasis on God's design also would have helped me learn more of the storyline of the Bible. Often the gospel presentation you hear as a teenager concludes with an invitation to say some magic words in a prayer that provides some sort of assurance that you'll go to heaven when you die. A picture of what the gospel actually is and what takes place in my relationship to Jesus as a result were never talked about at our rallies and events. The gospel was "Who doesn't want to go to hell?" and if you've raised your hand indicating such, pray this prayer after me. At a True Love Waits rally, the formula was pray this prayer and now follow these rules. Yet when Paul wanted to illustrate the beauty of the gospel story in his letter to the Ephesians, he chose the one flesh union first instituted by God at creation (and echoed by Jesus in Matthew 19): "For this reason a man will leave his father and mother and be joined to his wife, and the two will become one flesh. This mystery is profound, but I am talking about Christ and the church. To sum up, each one of you is to love his wife as himself, and the wife is to respect her husband" (Eph. 5:31–33).

God's design for marriage has a grand purpose other than pro-creation, and it is to point us to the grandest marriage, the one between Christ and the church. Rather than rules, we see glory. It is absolutely incredible that when God created Adam and Eve for each other, He already had the gospel in mind. As a teenager, I wonder how I would have responded to hearing the story of marriage through the lens of biblical theology. Perhaps I would have seen the sexual ethics of the Bible as more than a list of rules to not mess up while also understanding the true weight of sex. I was taught the rules of sex but not the story of sex. With my own children today, I try to focus on the "what" and "why" of God's design rather than simply the prohibitions. I try to emphasize why God's design is good and clearly state the consequences of departing from His design. I want them to know that marriage isn't random or just a customary milestone—it is a mirror to the world of the relationship between Christ and the church. Rather than purity rings on their fingers, I want to see them have pure hearts.

I wish True Love Waits would have made its mission clearly about Jesus. I'm not suggesting the people behind the movement didn't love and follow Jesus; I just look back in sadness and disappointment that the gospel story was missing from the main presentation. It wasn't that we never heard the name of Jesus, but He wasn't given to us as the ultimate motivation for why we should "save ourselves" for marriage. What a lost opportunity to hold up Christ and make much of God's design for an age group who could have been taught so much about their Creator and what He has provided for His people. The reason for God's boundaries regarding sex are based on His glory and His grace.

2. THE RAMIFICATIONS

True Love Waits certainly did not shy away from being honest about the consequences of taking sex outside of God's purposes and design. They weren't exaggerating or fearmongering. Sexual sin leads to brokenness, and our sex-obsessed world is evidence of this reality. The amount of pain in our society that is a direct result of refusing to place our lives under God's design for sex is beyond measure. Yet the consequences of sexual sin do not include unending shame for those who are in Christ. As we rightly tell of the consequences of sin, it is critical to drive home the gospel truth that one does not have to live under the banner of shame, but rather, through repentance, under the forgiveness and acceptance of Christ.

Sexual sin does not leave one outside the camp of God's grace, but it should bring about personal conviction. This conviction is an act of God's grace, pointing us away from the world and to Himself. True Love Waits presented the main consequence as disappointing a future spouse. Past sexual sin can bring pain and hurt to a marriage, but that is not the primary consequence of sexual sin. Our sin is against the real God who has made Himself known to us, not against a hypothetical spouse whose name we don't even know. There is nothing hypothetical about our God. He has spoken "at different times and in different ways," and ultimately He has spoken to us by His Son (Heb. 1:1–2). The Christian's motivation for sexual purity should be growing in knowledge of and love for God.

Let me put this another way. Sin is deceptive, and all married people who have ever committed a sexual sin against their spouse have probably had the consequences of losing their marriage or family cross their mind. Yet they sinned anyway. So, if the reality of hurting your spouse, possibly losing your marriage, and only seeing your kids fifty percent of the time isn't enough, why would we think that it's sufficient to tell teenagers with raging hormones that they shouldn't have sex outside of marriage because it might hurt someone they might be married to one day, years down the road, whom they have never met? In an earthly sense, an unmarried teenager has less to ruin than a married father of three. Yet the ramifications of sexual sin are not first and foremost about losing your family or getting pregnant or ruining your reputation; they are about God and sinning against Him. If the fact that God already sees and knows is less on our minds than a plan to make sure no one else ever finds out, we will never overcome temptation and will fail miserably.

The greatest consequence of sexual sin is a severed relationship with the One against whom that sin is committed—God Himself. I wish that True Love Waits would have emphasized the holiness of God over the disappointment of a potential future spouse. God must be the reason above any other reason; otherwise our worship becomes misplaced. As a Christian, I will only be faithful as

> **The greatest consequence of sexual sin is a severed relationship with the One against whom that sin is committed— God Himself.**

a husband to the extent that I am faithful as a child of God. Peter wrote to the church, "As obedient children, do not be conformed to the desires of your former ignorance. But as the one who called you is holy, you also are to be holy in all your conduct; for it is written, Be holy, because I am holy" (1 Peter 1:14–16). A call to holiness is not legalism; it is the way of the distinct people of a distinct God. The opposite of holy living (according to Peter) is to be conformed to your former life, when you didn't know God or His Word. We are called to respond to the new life God has given us and to our adoption as His children by living as obedient children under His loving fatherhood. Unless I love God more than I love my wife and kids, family won't be a sufficient motivation for living in righteousness concerning sex. If I love God, I will keep His commandments, more concerned with what He thinks than with any other factor.

Paul told the Galatian Christians, "I have been crucified with Christ, and I no longer live, but Christ lives in me. The life I now live in the body, I live by faith in the Son of God, who loved me and gave himself for me" (Gal. 2:20). The call of the Christian is to no longer live for ourselves but rather live our lives by faith in Christ. One thing that resonates with younger Christians is the call to live their lives for Jesus. I remember as a teen leaving summer camps and retreats so excited to live for Christ and make His name known. How great would it have been if the True Love Waits rallies I attended motivated me to live for the Lord rather than follow the rules and not make myself into damaged goods for a future spouse. The great news for all is that "where sin multiplied, grace multiplied even more" (Rom. 5:20). The holiness of God should point us to the love of God and as a result cause our affections to grow for the One who first loved us.

3. THE RESOLVE

Amidst a culture of sexual chaos, Christians must live with strengthened resolve regarding their convictions. Coming of age during the True Love Waits era, I had no idea what awaited my generation when it came to believing and living out the sexual ethics as prescribed by God in Scripture. At True Love Waits rallies, we were told what not to do but never (in my recollection at least) equipped for what it was going to be like to live in the world with Christian convictions. We would be mocked, ridiculed, and shamed for having beliefs said to be harmful to others. We would be labeled bigots. That is a lot for a sixteen-year-old to handle. To be fair—and I believe this is an important clarification—it isn't the job of a rally or a parachurch movement to equip kids to live for Christ in the world. The responsibility rests on parents and the local church. But what is happening in the larger Christian culture usually trickles down to the local church. When speaking about sex, student ministries in local churches took the approach of True Love Waits and focused on prevention. It was churches who drove their buses to True Love Waits events, where the win for the ministry following the event was how many kids signed pledge cards.

It is astonishing to see how many people who signed those cards and were raised during that movement have abandoned their views on biblical sexual ethics, especially when it comes to gender and homosexuality. Students of our day have the status of first-century lepers if they profess Christian convictions regarding sex among their peers and in the halls of their schools. We must equip students to navigate this environment if we desire to see a generation hold to biblical orthodoxy in the future. What one does with the Bible's teaching on sexuality is now becoming an indication of where he or she will eventually land regarding faith in general. If you abandon what the Scriptures say regarding marriage being between a man and a woman, why shouldn't you also abandon what it says regarding the exclusivity of the saving work of Jesus Christ? Students must be taught resolve regarding their convictions and be encouraged to bravely live them out. When fellow students find out you are the girl who won't have a sexual relationship with your boyfriend, or when you're the guy who doesn't try to "get girls in bed," there are environments and social settings where you'll get made fun of, receive passive-aggressive comments, or be seen as an old-fashioned goodie-two-shoes (and that's probably the nicest thing you'd get called). That is a lot for a kid to endure.

A modern trend in Evangelical life is a concept called "deconstruction." There are different facets of this phenomenon, but Paula Rinehart offers a description of it in the context of faith: "Doubt and disillusionment have become the new form of enlightenment. It somehow sounds more authentic to share our doubt than it is to share our faith with confidence. We watch thoughtful Christian leaders 'break free' from the faith itself, as though shaking off invisible shackles. And it unnerves us."[1] I cannot help but think of purity culture when I read Rinehart's words. Perhaps the prevalence of deconstruction is related to the supposed trauma and shame produced by purity culture during the formative years of so many Christians.

Churches must be willing to help those who have been disillusioned by the Christian subculture's approach to sexual ethics and those dealing with doubt caused by the unrelenting pressure of the world to conform to its gods. A faithful church must disciple people through their doubts, not for the sake of taking them away but in order to build believers up in the Scriptures so they are unashamed of the gospel and of what their God has said about all things, including sex, gender, and marriage. Rinehart adds that "the Scriptures never treat doubt as a virtue. But they do assume it will be part of experience in a fallen world and will drive us either from God or to God . . . To be disillusioned is no fun, but it does strip us of some illusions that we needed to let go. Old ideals get reshaped."[2] Helping others shape their minds around the words of the God who is the same yesterday, today, and forever is going to have much more lasting power than merely giving people a list of dos and don'ts and hoping they don't fail. People who are confident in God's Word will be willing to live for God and will have the resolve to withstand the onslaught of the world's values.

4. THE REFUTATION

It's also essential that Christians can refute the lies of this world. However adamant it is about its views, the world is confused— the biggest lie the world sells is two competing thoughts crammed into one value system. On the one hand we are told "it's just sex," but on the other hand we are told that sexual freedom is everything and any sort of guideline or limitation is oppressive and hateful. So, is sex not a big deal, or is sexual fulfillment the air the world breathes? How confusing! I wish the True Love Waits movement had given us a better answer than "don't do it." Christians should be both prudent and wise, able to see where the world's logic breaks down and that God's never does. Sex functions as a religion in our culture, with tenets like sex being about who you are, how you act, and what fills you.

The understanding of sexual identity in our age is like a god. Out of a love for our neighbor and a desire to see others reached for Christ, followers of Jesus must be able to both give the case for biblical sexual ethics and refute the lies of this world regarding sexuality. I believe the best way to do this is to provide answers for the three tenets of this religion of sex.

- **Sex is not "who you are."** One's identity is not found in his or her sexual desires or relational status but must ultimately be found in what he or she believes about Jesus Christ. The world cannot provide the answers many are looking for regarding their identity and purpose. Its best answer is that people are whatever they feel, especially regarding sexual desires, and should devote their lives to self-discovery regarding these things. If we want to see our friends reached for Christ, part of the conversation will have to be refuting the world's concept of identity.

- **Sex is not just how you act or the reason why you feel the way you feel and do the things you do.** People are told that they should act on whatever they feel, but feelings are unreliable. Yes, we should pay attention to our feelings, but we shouldn't let them call the shots. Far too often, when it comes to moral choices regarding sex and sexuality, the value system of this age encourages us to simply act based on how we feel. But the tragedy is that the world knows the heart is a bad compass. Even hit songs talk about regret, mistakes, and the heart leading us astray. There is a better guide! We must acknowledge the foolishness and self-centeredness of such a belief system and point people to rational truth from God's Word.

- **Sex is not the key to satisfaction and fulfillment.** Christians must also refute the false gospel of sexual fulfillment as an end in itself. This has become such a god in our culture that to not have one's desires met is seen as the ultimate oppression and deprivation. Often our desires are not unfulfilled but are rather misdirected.

To my sincerest recollection, the cultural narratives concerning sex were never refuted or even discussed at True Love Waits events or in any aspect of purity culture. The audience was simply pressed to treat sex before marriage like a "just say no" campaign against drugs from the 1980s. The result was a generation that bought purity rings and signed pledge cards but could not articulate God's design or give an answer to a world preaching the exact opposite message. Remaining faithful to our Christian convictions certainly takes resolve, but being on mission also includes questioning and refuting the gods of this world that are leading so many away from Jesus Christ. I wish the True Love Waits movement would have had a missional component (that actually stuck) beyond keeping people from doing something they might regret. To reach a sexually broken world, Christians must go beyond simply telling people what to do and instead speak to the insufficiency of the gods and values of a fading and unfulfilling world.

14

Words for the Broken

"And some of you used to be like this. But you were washed,
you were sanctified, you were justified in the name of the Lord Jesus
Christ and by the Spirit of our God."

1 CORINTHIANS 6:11

These are some of the most beautiful words in the entire Bible, strung together in just one verse. To those who have lived their lives in sin or have crossed the threshold of impurity, Paul makes it clear: if you are in Christ, that's not who you are anymore. It's not just that Paul's readers stopped doing something and "used to be like this." They were washed, and this wash made them spotless and sanctified—holy before God. This took place in their being declared not guilty and completely righteous by justification. Philip Eveson defines this doctrine as "God's gracious judicial verdict in advance of the day of judgment, pronouncing guilty sinners, who turn in self-despairing trust to Jesus Christ, forgiven, acquitted of all charges and declared morally upright in God's sight."[1] Consider the implications of this amazing verse for all of us who have not only sinned but still feel the shame and guilt of past choices. Not only are we forgiven of our sins, which is an unthinkable act of God's amazing grace, but we are declared morally upright.

I have a polo shirt with a grease stain from some time ago. To this day, after trying every washing remedy imaginable, the spot is still there. It is common for people who understand they've been forgiven of their sins by the blood of Jesus Christ to believe they still carry a stain on their lives. Even though they believe God cleanses sin, they think they still have that greasy spot. The apostle Paul, writing under the inspiration of the Holy Spirit, has a word for someone who thinks that way: you have been washed and that stain is ancient history. Unlike the grease on my shirt, your guilt does not exist anymore. We might still feel it, but God does not see it.

At True Love Waits rallies, the testimonies were usually from people who had had sex before marriage and regretted it. I understood that these people were forgiven by Christ, but I also felt bad for them because they seemed to carry so much guilt and shame. As I look back now, I hope that those who repented of sexual sin and shared their testimonies would go on to believe the implications of their justification in Jesus Christ. Yes, the effects of our sin will still linger in this world, but we should refuse to see ourselves differently than how God sees us. To do so would suggest that His washing didn't accomplish what it was intended to do. Dan Dewitt says that "we must deal with our shame by reminding ourselves of how God has dealt with our guilt."[2] The remedy to our self-condemnation is to look to our justification. Dewitt adds, "Our guilt is objectively forgiven at the cross. In Christ, God has cast our sin as far as the east is from the west (Ps. 103:12). But shame will refuse to acknowledge our new identity. May we not let it have the last word."[3]

The lingering effects we feel from past choices come from brokenness. In the way I'm using it here, brokenness is different than sinning, which must always be seen as an offense against God. Instead, brokenness is a word used to describe the effects of sin. When we go outside of God's design, things break, and those cracks can be repaired as we recover and pursue God's way and follow His commands in faith. Yes, some consequences remain long past our forgiveness, but God has provided means for us to begin to repair what has been broken. The blood of Jesus Christ shed in our place on the cross is what cleanses our sin, but the consequences of our choices can function more as an aftershock.

The path out of brokenness must begin with biblical community. Get involved in a grace-filled, Bible-committed local church, into a family and environment where, since God does not count our sins against us, fellow believers also refuse to do so. Along with commitment to a local body of believers, I strongly recommend Christian counseling to help sort through the hurts of the past and build a plan to walk forward in life as a new creation. As I have mentioned, departing from God's design leaves real brokenness in its wake, and thankfully God has provided resources such as counseling to help in the aftermath. Third, I believe there is healing power in fully embracing your new life, looking not to what is behind, but what is ahead (see Phil. 3:13). Whether that means having a marriage that honors God or a completely new approach to friendships with the opposite sex and dating, the new life committed to pursuing God's design is one you can feel excited about.

If you are ministering to someone in or coming out of sexual sin, or find yourself living in it, know that a central theme of the New Testament is Jesus meeting us in our brokenness. One such example is the story of the woman at the well in John chapter four. In this encounter, Jesus walked into Samaria, a place avoided by Jews due to the alleged uncleanness of the Samaritan people. By entering the town of Samaria, Jesus displayed that He didn't operate according to the way of the religious of His time. It is the spiritually sick who need a doctor, and the Great Physician was about to make His own house call, bringing the medicine of His grace. Once in Samaria, Jesus stopped at Jacob's Well, since He was worn out from His journey. John includes the seemingly random detail that "it was about noon." But at this time, "a woman of Samaria came to draw water" (John 4:6–7).

A study of the culture of Samaria during this time period would show that noon is not a normal time to get water. It might make sense to go at noon for the purpose of beating the crowd, like when I head to a busy restaurant for lunch at 11:15 instead of noon to avoid the lines. But after a brief conversation about physical water and thirst, the story flips and we see exactly what is going on and what it is that John wants us to understand.

> "Go call your husband," he told her, "and come back here."
> "I don't have a husband," she answered.
> "You have correctly said, 'I don't have a husband,'" Jesus said. "For you've had five husbands, and the man you now have is not your husband. What you have said is true." (John 4:16–18)

That must be on the list of top five most awkward moments in the history of conversation. Imagine that moment. But what seems like a haymaker of judgment from Jesus is actually an invitation into grace. He doesn't bring up her past relationship failures and current living status in order to condemn her but to offer her a different way, one that she knew she needed. The woman didn't arrive early at the well because she didn't want to wait long but because she didn't want to be seen. It was no secret she had been married five times or that the man she was now with wasn't her husband. The comments, stares, and gossip were likely too much to handle. While she didn't want to be seen by others, Jesus wanted her to know that He could see her clearly. In fact, He came to Samaria just to see her.

In that moment, Jesus wasn't willing to send her back to continue living in sin or let her remain at her incognito noontime shame. After He revealed to her that He was indeed the Messiah she had been told about and was hoping for, John tells us, "Many Samaritans from that town

> My prayer is that every person living in sexual sin has a Jacob's Well encounter with Jesus, where sin gets confronted not with shame but with grace.

believed in him because of what the woman said when she testified, 'He told me everything I ever did'" (John 4:39). Normally, if someone told you everything you had ever done and in the context of your sin, the last thing you would do is celebrate. But here this woman celebrated this encounter not as someone who was creeped out or judged but as someone who was finally free.

The life of the woman at the well was marked by brokenness, but now, she would be washed by living water. We aren't told exactly what happened in the rest of her life, but we do know that she met Jesus and rejoiced because of it. Jesus directly addressed her sins, and the spiritual water He gave her was everything she ever needed. My prayer is that every person living in sexual sin has a Jacob's Well encounter with Jesus, where sin gets confronted not with shame but with grace. Jesus sees you and isn't looking with disapproval. He walks into your town, into your noontime hiding, and offers you a water that will quench your thirst and satisfy your soul.

Our world is quick to accuse God's design as oppressive. I wish those making this claim could ask the woman from the well (I am going to find out her name when I get to heaven) exactly what oppression looks like. I bet she'd say that being a slave to her desires and circumstances was the oppressive weight, and that the man named Jesus showed her a path of complete and true freedom. God's design wasn't outdated for her either; it got to her just in time. May the scene at Jacob's Well be the future of our ministry when it comes to receiving those who are broken by sexual sin. Let's turn purity culture into gospel culture. Rather than signing a card pledging your purity, God makes a pledge to all who receive Him by faith, and that promise is Himself.

Notes

CHAPTER 1—PURITY CULTURE & "TRUE LOVE WAITS"

1. Joe Carter, "The FAQ's: What You Should Know about Purity Culture," The Gospel Coalition, July 24, 2019, https://www.thegospelcoalition.org/article/faqs-know-purity-culture/.
2. Angie Hong, "The Flaw at the Center of Purity Culture," The Atlantic, March 28, 2021, https://www.theatlantic.com/ideas/archive/2021/03/purity-culture-evangelical-church-harms-women/618438/.
3. Sandi Villareal, "Their Generation Was Shamed By Purity Culture, Here's What They're Building in its Place," Sojourners, March 7, 2019, https://sojo.net/interactive/their-generation-was-shamed-purity-culture-heres-what-theyre-building-its-place.
4. Katelyn Beaty, "How Should Christians Have Sex?," The New York Times, June 15, 2019, https://www.nytimes.com/2019/06/15/opinion/sunday/sex-christian.html.
5. "A Timeline of HIV and AIDS," HIV.gov, https://www.hiv.gov/hiv-basics/overview/history/hiv-and-aids-timeline.
6. "Adolescent Health," OASH Office of Public Affairs, https://opa.hhs.gov/adolescent-health?adolescent-development/reproductive-health-and-teen-pregnancy/teen-pregnancy-and-childbearing/trends/index.html.
7. Carter, "The FAQ's: What You Should Know About Purity Culture."
8. Original source has been updated or removed, but many news articles from the era cite the original language, including this one from 1993: Lisa Daniels, "True Love Waits," Daily Press, November 21, 1993, https://www.dailypress.com/news/dp-xpm-19931121-1993-11-21-9311210122-story.html.

9. True Love Waits was started by Richard Ross, through Lifeway Christian Resources. An idea he proposed in 1992 for a campaign to promote sexual purity for students.

10. Carter, "The FAQ's: What You Should Know About Purity Culture."

11. Kathy Keller, *New City Catechism: 52 Questions and Answers for Our Hearts and Minds* (Wheaton, IL: Crossway, 2017).

12. Paul Carter, "What is Sin?," The Gospel Coalition, December 20, 2019, https://ca.thegospelcoalition.org/columns/ad-fontes/what-is-sin/.

13. Beaty, "How Should Christians Have Sex?"

14. Erin Roach, "At Song's Anniversary, Rebecca St. James Revisits 'Wait for Me,'" *Baptist Press*, April 5, 2006, https://www.baptistpress.com/resource-library/news/at-songs-anniversary-rebecca-st-james-revisits-wait-for-me/.

15. Beaty, "How Should Christians Have Sex?"

CHAPTER 2—PURITY CULTURE & "I KISSED DATING GOODBYE"

1. Joshua Harris, *I Kissed Dating Goodbye* (Colorado Springs: Multnomah, 2003).

2. Directed and produced by Jessica Van Der Wyngaard in conjunction with Joshua Harris. DOCSology Pty Ltd, 2018. https://www.youtube.com/watch?v=ybYTkkQJw_M.

3. Harris, *I Kissed Dating Goodbye*, 13–14.

4. Shoutout to Gary Chapman.

5. Betsy Childs Howard, *Seasons of Waiting: Walking by Faith When Dreams Are Delayed* (Wheaton, IL: Crossway, 2016).

CHAPTER 3—THE COUNTER SWING TO "IT'S JUST SEX"

1. Richard E. Simmons III, "Sex at First Sight: Understanding the Modern Hookup Culture," *Rooted Ministry*, June 13, 2015, https://www.rootedministry.com/blog/sex-at-first-sight-understanding-the-modern-hookup-culture/.

2. John Murray, *Redemption Accomplished and Applied* (Grand Rapids: Eerdmans, 1955), 161.

3. Justin Taylor, "Union with Christ: A Crash Course," The Gospel Coalition, February 10, 2011, https://www.thegospelcoalition.org/blogs/justin-taylor/union-with-christ-a-crash-course/.

4. Tony Reinke, "Union with Christ," personal website, March 13, 2010, https://tonyreinke.com/2010/03/13/union-with-christ/.

SECTION 2— PASSING THROUGH: LIVING AS EXILES IN A SEX-CRAZED WORLD

1. Tim Keller, via Twitter, April 24, 2021, thread beginning with https:// twitter.com/timkellernyc/status/1385951866660474886?lang=en.

2. Tim Keller, via Twitter, April 24, 2021: https://twitter.com/timkellernyc/ status/1385951871811170304.

CHAPTER 4—LIE NO. 1: "SEX IS EXPECTED"

1. "Hookup," APA Dictionary of Psychology, https://dictionary.apa.org/ hookup.

2. Leah Fessler, "A Lot of Women Don't Enjoy Hookup Culture, So Why Do We Force Ourselves to Participate," Quartz, May 17, 2016, https:// qz.com/685852/hookup-culture/.

CHAPTER 5—LIE NO. 2: "MARRIAGE IS A CAPSTONE, NOT A CORNERSTONE"

1. I first heard pastor Jimmy Scroggins use the terminology that marriage should be a cornerstone and not a capstone. I've reversed his metaphor here to reflect the world's mindset.

2. The Editors of Encyclopaedia Britannica, "cornerstone," Encyclopedia Britannica, https://www.britannica.com/technology/cornerstone.

CHAPTER 6—LIE NO. 3: "PORN IS THE NORM"

1. David Powlison, "Breaking Pornography Addiction," CCEF, October 16, 2009, https://www.ccef.org/breaking-pornography-addiction-part-1/.

2. Kevin DeYoung, "I Don't Understand Christians Watching Game of Thrones," The Gospel Coalition, August 8, 2017, https://www.thegospel coalition.org/blogs/kevin-deyoung/i-dont-understand-christians- watching-game-of-thrones/.

3. Kevin DeYoung, "One More Time on 'Game of Thrones,'" The Gospel Coalition, August 22, 2017, https://www.thegospelcoalition.org/blogs/ kevin-deyoung/one-more-time-on-game-of-thrones/.

4. Ibid.

5. Ibid.

6. Ibid.

7. Ibid.

8. Megan Hill, "The Modesty Conversation We Need to Have," The Gospel Coalition, June 29, 2021, https://www.thegospelcoalition.org/article/modesty-conversation/.

9. Ibid.

10. Ibid.

11. Ibid.

12. Elisabeth Elliot, *Let Me Be a Woman* (Carol Stream, IL: Tyndale House, 1999).

13. Hill, "The Modesty Conversation We Need to Have."

14. Sam Allberry, "5 Myths about Body Image," Crossway, August 3, 2021, https://www.crossway.org/articles/5-myths-about-body-image/.

15. Hill, "The Modesty Conversation We Need to Have."

CHAPTER 7—LIE NO. 4: "GAY IS OKAY"

1. Macklemore, Ryan Lewis, Mary Lambert, "Same Love." *The Heist*, 2012.

2. https://www.churchclarity.org/about.

3. Gene Burrus, "My Hope for Spiritual Friendship and Revoice," *Intersect Project*, August 22, 2018, https://intersectproject.org/faith-and-culture/hope-spiritual-friendship-revoice/.

4. Ibid.

5. Steven Wedgeworth, "A Critical Review of Spiritual Friendship," *Mere Orthodoxy*, June 12, 2018, https://mereorthodoxy.com/critical-review-spiritual-friendship/.

6. Jackie Hill Perry, "I Loved My Girlfriend—But God Loved Me More," *Christianity Today*, August 20, 2018, https://www.christianitytoday.com/ct/2018/september/jackie-hill-perry-gay-girl-good-god.html.

7. Ibid.

8. Ibid.

CHAPTER 8—LIE NO. 5:
"MY BEDROOM IS MY BUSINESS"

1. "Sexperiment," Ed Young, https://www.edyoung.com/books/sexperiment.

2. Ibid.

3. "Pastor Challenges Congregation to Seven Days of Sex," NBC Dallas Fort-Worth, November 10, 2008, https://www.nbcdfw.com/news/national-international/pastor-challenges-congregation-to-seven-days-of-sex/1843264/.

4. Sonia Smith, "Bum Steer: Grapevine Pastor Ed Young Plans 24-Hour 'Bed-In' on Roof of Church," *Texas Monthly*, January 11, 2012, https://www.texasmonthly.com/articles/bum-steer-grapevine-pastor-ed-young-plans-24-hour-bed-in-on-roof-of-church/.

5. Mark Driscoll and Grace Driscoll, *Real Marriage: The Truth about Sex, Friendship, and Life Together* (Nashville: Thomas Nelson, 2013), 177.

6. Samuel Parkison, "CT's The Rise and Fall of Mars Hill: An Inquiry," personal website, July 28, 2021, https://samuelparkison.wordpress.com/2021/07/28/cts-the-rise-and-fall-of-mars-hill-an-inquiry/.

7. Mike Cosper, "The Things We Do To Women," *Christianity Today*, July 26, 2021, https://www.christianitytoday.com/ct/podcasts/rise-and-fall-of-mars-hill/mars-hill-mark-driscoll-podcast-things-we-do-women.html.

8. Mark Driscoll, "The Man," Acts 29 Bootcamp, Raleigh, NC, September 20, 2007.

9. Craig Welch, "The Rise and Fall of Mars Hill Church," *Seattle Times*, originally posted September 13, 2014 and updated February 4, 2016, https://www.seattletimes.com/seattle-news/the-rise-and-fall-of-mars-hill-church/.

10. Beth Moore, *Twitter*, July 27, 2021, https://twitter.com/bethmoorelpm/status/1420132100704030725?lang=en.

11. Rosie Moore, "6 Ingredients for Sexual Fulfilment in Marriage," The Gospel Coalition, January 26, 2021, https://africa.thegospelcoalition.org/article/6-ingredients-for-sexual-fulfilment-in-marriage/.

12. Douglas Sean O'Donnell, "The Earth Is Crammed with Heaven: Four Guideposts to Reading and Teaching the Song of Songs," Themelios, *Themelios* 37, no. 1, https://www.thegospelcoalition.org/themelios/article/the-earth-is-crammed-with-heaven-four-guideposts-to-reading-and-teaching-th/.

13. Kyle Dillon, "Is the Song of Songs about Sex or Jesus?," The Gospel Coalition, April 27, 2020, https://www.thegospelcoalition.org/article/song-songs-sex-or-jesus/.

14. Ibid.

15. Ibid.

CHAPTER 9—LIE NO. 6: "NOBODY HAS TO KNOW"

1. "Spiritual Adultery," Ligonier Ministries, September 8, 2010, https://www.ligonier.org/learn/devotionals/spiritual-adultery.

2. Ibid.

3. Samuel James, "Seeing Ourselves in 'The End of the Affair,'" The Gospel Coalition, August 17, 2017, https://www.thegospelcoalition.org/article/seeing-ourselves-in-the-end-of-the-affair/.

4. Willard F. Harley, Jr., His Needs, Her Needs: Building an Affair-Proof Marriage, revised ed. (Ada, MI: Baker Publishing Group, 2011).

5. Christopher Ash, Married for God: Making Your Marriage the Best It Can Be (Wheaton, IL: Crossway, 2016).

6. Some debate the legitimacy of this passage, as some of the oldest New Testament manuscripts do not include it. But, as John Calvin wrote concerning the story, it "contains nothing unworthy of an Apostolic Spirit, there is no reason why we should refuse to apply it to our advantage." ("The Woman Caught in Adultery," Ligonier Ministries, May 4, 2018, https://www.ligonier.org/learn/devotionals/woman-caught-in-adultery).

CHAPTER 10—LIE NO. 7: "COHABITATION JUST MAKES SENSE"

1. "cohabitation," Lexico, https://www.lexico.com/en/definition/cohabitation.

2. Juliana Menasce Horowitz, Nikki Graf, and Gretchen Livingston, "Marriage and Cohabitation in the U.S.," November 6, 2019, https://www.pewresearch.org/social-trends/2019/11/06/public-views-of-marriage-and-cohabitation/.

3. Arielle Kuperberg, "Does Premarital Cohabitation Raise Your Risk of Divorce?" Council on Contemporary Families, March 10, 2014, https://contemporaryfamilies.org/cohabitation-divorce-brief-report/.

4. I changed the names out of respect for the privacy of the couple.

5. David Shuman, "4 Reasons Not to Move in With Your Partner," The Gospel Coalition, March 1, 2021, https://www.thegospelcoalition.org/article/reasons-not-move-in-partner/.

6. Horowitz, Graf, and Livingston, "Marriage and Cohabitation in the U.S."

7. "Religious Landscape Study," Pew Research Center, https://www.pewforum.org/religious-landscape-study.

8. Erin Davis, "Should You Cohabitate Before Marriage?" ERLC, May 13, 2015, https://erlc.com/resource-library/articles/should-you-cohabitate-before-marriage/.

CHAPTER 11—TO THE WAITING: SINGLENESS AND THE GOSPEL

1. Katelyn Beaty, "How Should Christians Have Sex?" *The New York Times*, June 15, 2019, https://www.nytimes.com/2019/06/15/opinion/sunday/sex-christian.html.

2. Ibid.

3. Sam Allberry, via Twitter, Oct. 8, 2015, https://twitter.com/SamAllberry/status/652299545469059072.

4. Matt Smethurst, "9 Ways to Pastor Single Christians Longing for Marriage," The Gospel Coalition, May 15, 2018, https://www.thegospelcoalition.org/article/9-ways-pastor-single-christians-longing-marriage/.

5. "Gender Composition among Christians," Pew Research Center, https://www.pewforum.org/religious-landscape-study/christians/christian/#gender-composition.

6. "Belief in God among Christians by gender," Pew Research Center, https://www.pewforum.org/religious-landscape-study/christians/christian/gender-composition/#belief-in-god.

7. "Importance of religion in one's life among Christians by gender," Pew Research Center, https://www.pewforum.org/religious-landscape-study/christians/christian/gender-composition/#importance-of-religion-in-ones-life.

8. "Frequency of prayer among Christians by gender," Pew Research Center, https://www.pewforum.org/religious-landscape-study/christians/christian/gender-composition/#frequency-of-prayer-trend.

9. "Attendance at religious services among Christians by gender," Pew Research Center, https://www.pewforum.org/religious-landscape-

study/christians/christian/gender-composition/#attendance-at-religious-services.

10. Vaughan Roberts, "Vaughan Roberts on Singleness," *Living Out*, January 12, 2021, https://www.livingout.org/resources/articles/36/vaughan-roberts-on-singleness.

11. Attributed to Oscar Wilde.

12. Robert H. Mounce, *The Book of Revelation*, vol. 27 (Grand Rapids: Eerdmans, 1998), 266.

13. Brooks Waldron, "Singleness with a Purpose," The Gospel Coalition, November 17, 2010, https://www.thegospelcoalition.org/article/singleness-with-purpose/.

14. Tim Keller, "Creation's Groans are Not Meaningless," The Gospel Coalition, July 15, 2015, https://www.thegospelcoalition.org/article/creations-groans-are-not-meaningless/.

15. Vaughan Roberts, "Vaughan Roberts on Singleness."

CHAPTER 12—GOD GIVES A "WAY OUT"

1. Grace Thornton, "We Must 'Hunger and Thirst for Righteousness' Says Moore," *The Alabama Baptist*, September 13, 2019, https://thealabamabaptist.org/we-must-hunger-and-thirst-for-righteousness-says-moore/.

2. John Piper, "Man Shall Not Live on Bread Alone: What to Eat While Fasting," *Desiring God*, January 15, 1995, https://www.desiringgod.org/messages/man-shall-not-live-on-bread-alone.

3. Caedmon's Call, "Potiphar's Door." *The Guild Collection* (Volume 2), 1998.

CHAPTER 13—WHAT I WISH THE TRUE LOVE WAITS MOVEMENT WOULD HAVE TAUGHT ME

1. Paula Rinehart, "Dealing with Doubt in an Age of Deconstruction," The Gospel Coalition, August 9, 2019, https://www.thegospelcoalition.org/article/dealing-doubt-age-deconstruction/.

2. Ibid.

CHAPTER 14—WORDS FOR THE BROKEN

1. Philip Eveson, "The Doctrine of Justification," The Gospel Coalition, https://www.thegospelcoalition.org/essay/the-doctrine-of-justification/.

2. Dan Dewitt, "The Difference Between Guilt and Shame," The Gospel Coalition, February 19, 2018, https://www.thegospelcoalition.org/article/difference-between-guilt-shame/.

3. Ibid.

IS TRYING TO BE "THE BEST YOU" ACTUALLY RUINING YOU?

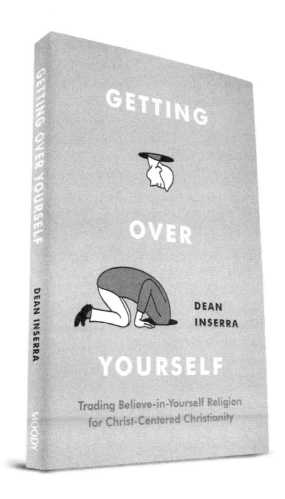

GETTING OVER YOURSELF

DEAN INSERRA

GETTING OVER YOURSELF

DEAN INSERRA

MOODY

Trading Believe-in-Yourself Religion for Christ-Centered Christianity

Getting Over Yourself is a call for Christians to reject the hollow messages of personal prosperity and to return to the humble truths of the gospel. You'll learn how to identify this insidious, popular theology in culture and churches and examine its devastating effects. You'll learn how to combat it with gospel truth that leads to the abundant life Jesus desires for His people.

978-0-8024-2307-8 | also available as eBook and audiobook

DOUBTING GOD IS NORMAL.
BUT CONFIDENCE IN HIM IS POSSIBLE.

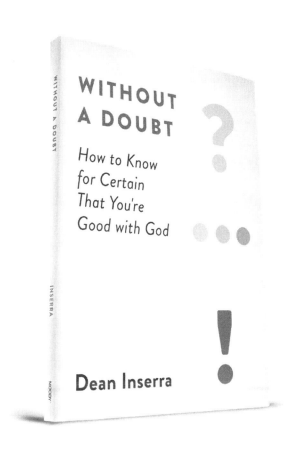

MOODY
Publishers®

From the Word to Life®

Without a Doubt is for anyone who wrestles with whether their faith is well-grounded or the promises of Christianity are true. Pastor Dean Inserra lays out what the Bible teaches about how to have saving faith in God. You'll learn the clear truth about what a Christian is—and what a Christian is not.

978-0-8024-2360-3 | also available as eBook and audiobook